## Acclaim for *How to Be a Girl*

"*How to Be a Girl* exemplifies the true meaning of unconditional love. In this book, Marlo learns that her 'son' is actually a transgender girl and, terrified at first, shows what it looks like to find acceptance and how transformative and uplifting that can be. Capturing the complexity of a mother's journey to understand her daughter, this book is universally relatable to any parent who is struggling to adapt and embrace who their child truly is as opposed to who the parent thought they were. As transgender children are often misunderstood, *How to Be a Girl* is an invaluable tool to providing the support and empathy they need. Marlo's tender reflection and courageous love is an inspiration that will help others to their own awakening."—JAZZ JENNINGS

"Marlo Mack's *How to Be a Girl* is an extraordinary mother-daughter story and also a wondrously ordinary one, not just about a mother's unconditional love but also about listening to one another, learning together, following your mama-gut as well as your mama-heart, and leaping into the unknown with a child—your child—as your guide." —LAURIE FRANKEL, New York Times–bestselling author of *This Is How It Always Is* and *One Two Three*

"The gender journey is beautiful, though lined with thorns. Marlo Mack brings this journey to life in exquisite, compassionate recollections. Her honesty and wide-angle lens make *How to Be a Girl* a brilliant must-read for any family member of a gender creative child and every ally and professional who wants to make this an affirming world for children of all genders. Thank you, Marlo Mack, for setting us on the right path in the journey."—DIANE EHRENSAFT, PhD, director of mental health, Child and Adolescent Gender Center, University of California Benioff Children's Hospital, and author of *The Gender Creative Child*

"Throughout *How to Be a Girl* are conversations about gender between Marlo and her child that would have been impossible within my own family. While society still struggles with its one-dimensional perspective of gender, Marlo Mack takes the reader through her tesseract-like journey to love, support, and celebrate her daughter. The end result? The impossible becomes possible, and we all have greater capacity to see the brilliant parenting path we once could never have imagined." —AIDAN KEY, gender educator, speaker, and author

# How to Be
# a Girl

# HOW TO BE A GIRL

## A Mother's Memoir of Raising Her Transgender Daughter

# MARLO MACK

THE EXPERIMENT

NEW YORK

## For M., who hung the moon

The Experiment, LLC
220 East 23rd Street, Suite 600
New York, NY 10010-4658
theexperimentpublishing.com

THE EXPERIMENT and its colophon are registered trademarks of The Experiment, LLC. Many of the designations used by manufacturers and sellers to distinguish their products are claimed as trademarks. Where those designations appear in this book and The Experiment was aware of a trademark claim, the designations have been capitalized.

The Experiment's books are available at special discounts when purchased in bulk for premiums and sales promotions as well as for fundraising or educational use. For details, contact us at info@theexperimentpublishing.com.

Library of Congress Cataloging-in-Publication Data

Names: Mack, Marlo, author.
Title: How to be a girl : a mother's memoir of raising her transgender daughter / Marlo Mack.
Description: New York : The Experiment, LLC, [2021]
Identifiers: LCCN 2021032847 (print) | LCCN 2021032848 (ebook) | ISBN 9781615197989 (paperback) | ISBN 9781615197996 (ebook)
Subjects: LCSH: Mack, Marlo. | Parents of transgender children--Biography. | Transgender children--Family relationships. | Mother and child. | Gender identity in children.
Classification: LCC HQ759.9147 .M33 2021 (print) | LCC HQ759.9147 (ebook) | DDC 306.76/8083 [B]--dc23
LC record available at https://lccn.loc.gov/2021032847
LC ebook record available at https://lccn.loc.gov/2021032848

ISBN 978-1-61519-798-9
Ebook ISBN 978-1-61519-799-6

Cover design by Beth Bugler
Cover photograph by Marlo Mack
Text design by Sarah Schneider

Manufactured in the United States of America

First printing October 2021
10 9 8 7 6 5 4 3 2 1

# CONTENTS

# Author's Note

The story I'm about to share with you is about real people. It's about me and my daughter and those who have lived through this very interesting time with us. To preserve the privacy of my child and others, I've changed nearly all of the names, including my own.

What I have not changed is the story, as I actually lived it. I'll be telling you this story from the beginning, which was ten long years ago, back in 2011. Back when I knew almost nothing about the profoundly complex and beautiful possibilities of gender; when I was the bewildered, doting mother of a precocious three-year-old who had so much to teach me.

**Me:** That's a beautiful drawing.

**My child (age three):** Yes, it is.

**Me:** Can you tell me about it?

**My child:** It's me and you, Mama.

**Me:** Which one is you?

**My child:** That's me. You're a princess. And I'm a fairy.

"A princess and a fairy," drawn by my three-year-old

# Take a deep breath.

There are not many moments like this. Moments that split open your world, slicing a deep crevasse across your life, so that everything before the moment belongs to a foreign, unvisitable world where a language is spoken that you no longer speak, and the words and customs of the new world are suddenly all that is comprehensible to you. It might happen after a big death, or the birth of your first child. Or it might be upon hearing a particular string of words uttered at that right, rare moment when your heart is raw and open.

That is what happened to me. I knew my child was different from the other children. I knew that most three-year-old boys did not spend long afternoons playing with plastic fairy figurines. I knew they didn't beg their moms for ballet classes and princess dresses and everything that sparkled and glittered. I knew this was going to be more complicated, raising a boy who did not act like one.

The other moms assured me it would pass. At preschool pickup, they would enthusiastically compliment the surprisingly pink shoes worn by my little boy. "What a fun color!" a mom would say. And as my son smiled shyly and looked down to admire his beautiful feet, the mother of an older boy would tell me of the time when her own son had likewise mistaken the world of girls for his own. "My son loved pink in preschool, too!" she might say. Or "He used to dress up in his big sister's clothes!" She would laugh at her sweet story, an example of the kind of charming error small children often make, like thinking you could draw your own money, or that your parents were old enough to remember the dinosaurs.

But I wondered.

I wondered if her son had ever drawn a self-portrait with puff-sleeved gowns and Rapunzel-length hair. Or recoiled at the sound of his own name, declaring it ugly and pleading to instead be called something pretty, like Rainbow. I wondered if her son had ripped off his clothes every day after school, to replace them with the floral-print party dress coaxed out of his grandma on a trip to the thrift store, and if he had then twirled around the living room in a graceful trance, singing a tuneless song about fairies.

I wondered if this mother had dithered and delayed in response to his ever-pinker requests, hoping this unusual passion would subside with time. If she had lain awake at night wondering where she had gone wrong, asking herself how she had so utterly failed to steer her precious boy in a safer direction, and whether there was any chance left of helping him change course now.

And I wondered how she felt when it dawned on her that all of the characters in her son's favorite books, and the only children he requested for playdates, and every single one of his beloved stuffed animals . . . were girls.

Like me, she had probably never heard of a boy like that—a boy who didn't seem to want to be one.

My child's self-portrait, age four

When the world split wide open, it was a November evening. We had just walked in the front door and were shedding the day's damp coats and bags. Outside, the Seattle sky was preparing for an early bedtime, transforming the cloud ceiling from old-pillow gray to the color of wet ash.

I reached out to flip on the lights and felt my child slip his hand into mine.

"Mama," he said, "something went wrong in your tummy."

I heard my purse hit the floor. "It did?"

"Yes," he said. "And it made me come out as a boy instead of a girl."

The tips of his fingers dug into my palm, and I looked down at the three-year-old face tilted up at mine. The perfect brow was creased down the middle. His pale blue eyes, like circles cut from a summer sky, were flooding with tears, but did not blink. His little body, usually in constant motion, was unnaturally rigid and tall, a tiny soldier frozen at attention.

"Breathe," I said to both of us. "Take a deep breath."

He ignored me. "Put me back, Mama," he rasped, expelling all that was left in his little lungs. "Put me back, so I can come out again as a girl." He gasped for air and his body curled up into sobs. I sank to my knees and reached for him, but he pushed me away and pointed with his whole arm at my stomach. "Please, Mama!" my child howled. "Put me back!"

The evening's last gray light was gone, the living room windows had turned black, and the door to the kitchen was now a bright rectangle filling the room with long shadows, including ours, which climbed the wall to the same height, and which were both trembling.

For months, I had been saying no to requests well within my power to grant: sundresses and ballet slippers and Barbie dolls. But now, my child was asking for something I couldn't possibly deliver. Now, the only reasonable answer to give, unequivocally, was no. And I could not.

I could say no to all those pretty objects, but not to this. Because whatever this was, I knew that it was real, and it was everything. It was the thing he had been trying to tell me, and that I had been trying not to see, for months, despite ten thousand sparkly hints. It was impossible, but somehow it was also true.

I bundled him into my lap and heard myself promise my child something I had no confidence that I could ever deliver. "It's OK," I said. "You can be a girl."

I held his damp head pressed against my heart and rocked him back and forth. He sniffed and shook in my arms while I continued to promise the impossible. "Yes, my darling. Yes."

We were a single swaying shadow on the wall now, and we rocked and rocked, until his tears were dry and one of us felt safe again.

I NOW LIVED UNDER the daily weight of my impossible promise. Although I had been unable to say *no*, I also had no idea what saying *yes* actually meant. There was no way, that I could see, to actually keep my promise. A boy could not become a girl. I may as well have agreed to let him become a *T. rex* or a slice of toast.

The few friends I told got very quiet. They had never heard of a child saying such a thing, either.

When I told my mom what my child had said about returning to my tummy, she just sighed. Three grown children and nearly seventy years on the planet had not prepared her for a child like mine. "This is a new one to me, honey," she said. "Have you told Will?"

I had not yet told Will, my child's father. A few months earlier, our fifteen-year relationship had quietly crumbled, and our initially peaceful parting had devolved into a stereotypical brawl over the disentangling of two long-entwined lives. For the moment, our child spent most of the time with me and stayed at his dad's new apartment a couple of nights each week. We were too angry at each other to discuss anything besides the basic logistics of co-parenting. So . . . no, I had not yet told my child's father that our son wanted a do-over in my womb.

My child wanted to be a slice of toast, and I was all alone.

❖

WHEN MY CHILD FIRST BEGAN venturing into the world of girls soon after he learned to walk and talk, his dad and I had pushed back—gently, we thought—cunningly employing various forms of the classic parental dodge: *Maybe later. We'll see. Those are too expensive.*

When I caved and bought my child the bicycle helmet he badly wanted—a pale pink one, decorated with a family of bunnies—Will got annoyed. I could tell he thought I'd been weak, and I agreed with him.

I thought, surely those moms at preschool were right. Surely this was a cute and harmless phase, and soon enough he would wake up to the undeniable fact of his boyhood and start selecting from among the trappings of his true tribe: rough games played with balls, noisy toys that had wheels and gears, clothing in dark, muted colors. And besides, Will and I said to each other, we were just being practical: It simply wasn't economical to invest in all the equipment of the wrong gender, only to replace it once our child woke up to who he actually was.

We did not say aloud the other things, the darker thoughts, that troubled us: If he kept going on this path, what would become of him? Who would accept him? Understand him? Love him? What would the world do to a boy like this?

If we could just coach him, *coax* him, into his boyness, perhaps we could save him from himself.

I scheduled playdates with little boys from preschool, though he never mentioned any of the boys—only the girls. I had to ask the teacher for the boys' names and track down their parents. I looked into karate classes and tried to drum up enthusiasm by reminding him that his dad had once earned a black belt. I invited my sister to come over regularly with her two sons. They were slightly older than my child, and these few extra years imbued them with an older-kid glamour their younger cousin found irresistible. This cousin-worship gave me a slight hope. Perhaps he would begin to see himself in these boyish little gods and aspire to become like them. The three cousins would wrestle and roughhouse and sword fight with sticks, and when I watched them I felt a little easing around my heart.

But in the pile of writhing arms and legs on my living room floor, the smallest pair of limbs were sheathed in shades of pink. And when the wrestling stopped, the youngest child went hunting for a princess dress and insisted it was time for a tea party.

Ultimately all our delays and dodges, our nudges and suggestions, failed completely. In spite of us, our child gradually amassed a wardrobe begged and borrowed from the girl world, the world with the things he loved. A lavender skirt fished out of a bag of hand-me-downs from a neighbor. A pink cardigan left behind by a visiting girl cousin. And the delightful spoils of his trips to the thrift store with Grandma, who didn't see any good reason to say no to that two-dollar sundress, those sparkle-spattered T-shirts, that jeweled tiara.

"Oh, what's the harm?" Grandma said. "When it gives him such joy?"

By the time his father moved out, just before the holidays and his fourth birthday, my child had purged his wardrobe of the last traces of boyhood and transformed himself into the pinkest child at preschool.

The moms who had once remarked so heartily on my boy's unlikely pink shoes went quiet. Their own sons never took it this far.

◈

Age three

IT WAS JUST WARM ENOUGH to be outside. I was on hands and knees in the backyard, pulling winter's weeds from a muddy flower bed. My child crouched nearby, perched like a bird atop hot-pink rubber rain boots, examining the pile of small, smooth stones he had spent the past hour collecting. I stopped weeding to watch as he picked up one of the stones, caressed it with his thumb, and put it back in the pile before choosing another that appeared identical. This one seemed to pass muster, and he laid it to the side in a weedless patch of dirt, then turned back to the pile to make another silent calculation. The chosen stones moved one by one until they formed a perfect circle, evenly spaced. Then he stood, hands on hips, and invited me to admire his work.

"Isn't it beautiful, Mama?"

"Yes, it's beautiful."

A breeze tossed his wispy hair, the same almost-blond shade as mine. It was an unruly length, climbing over the tops of his ears and getting mixed up in his eyebrows because he had refused to let me cut it ever again, "now that I'm going to be a girl."

Nodding at his circle of stones, he explained, "It is for the garden fairies. They do their magic here."

I crawled in for a closer look. "Really? What magic?"

"Geesh, Mama!" He threw up his arms at my ignorance. "Fairy magic! Beauty and flowers!" He asked if we could go inside and make a fairy potion.

I hoisted him up onto the kitchen counter and poured some water and a little cooking oil into a bowl and handed him a spoon. He wondered aloud what colors mix to make purple and then remembered, then asked for help unscrewing the caps on the red and blue food coloring. Before I could stop him, he had squirted in half of each bottle. The spoon swirled the potion into a deep oily purple.

Back outside, he scooped purple teaspoonfuls from the bowl and bent down to pour precise magic over each small stone, making his way halfway around the circle. Then he stood and declared, "That's enough," and dumped the remainder in the circle's center, creating a black puddle and splashing purple dots onto our boots.

I thought: *He is four years old, and fairies are real. As real as the pale spring leaves unfurling on the maple tree branches arched over our heads and the damp grass under our boots. As real as the two of us, mother and child, bending over this circle of pebbles, splattered in purple magic.*

"Now all the fairies will be happy," he announced. "And they can have all their wishes."

❖

MY PARENTS CAME OVER to help with spring cleaning in the garden. While Dad mowed the lawn, Mom pulled weeds and admired the fairy circle, careful not to disturb it. She helped gather more stones for a second ring. My child proclaimed that it was now a fairy city.

That evening he directed the three adults into seated silence in the living room while he performed an elaborate and elegant dance, wrapped in a sheer lavender scarf and nothing else. We applauded heartily.

When we sat down for dinner, I complained about my job and told my parents that I was thinking of getting a roommate to help pay the bills.

Dad said, "You be careful about who you let move in here, with my daughter and my precious grandson!"

My child contemplated his plate of buttered noodles and said, "I wish I could drink a potion that would make my penis melt off." Then he smiled, looking pleased with his great idea, like when he had suggested we build him a bed out of LEGOs.

The adults chewed in silence.

After dinner, Dad pulled me aside and asked if my child was spending enough time with his father. He was. Every week. And even though my interactions with my ex were brief and frosty, with his child Will was warm and attentive and playful. But I knew what people would think: *His dad just left and now he wants to be a girl.*

And I knew exactly how I would respond: *My child has loved the world of girls since his first wordless encounters with it. Before he had names for it, he cried out for it, he crawled toward it.* But of course, I too wondered and worried: Was my father right? Could these two events somehow be related?

**Me:** What things are "girl things?"

**My child (age four):** Ballerinas, pink and purple, jewelry . . . and dancing on a stage.

**Me:** Can *boys* dance on a stage?

**My child:** Only if they're getting married, like a prince.

It occurred to me that perhaps, and very probably, we were getting all stirred up over a misunderstanding. Surely this was really just a problem of definitions, of semantics, of the limitations of the available categories.

I decided that we needed to expand the definition of boyhood, one that included what he loved. One that included him.

My own childhood took place in the androgynous 1970s. With my bowl-cut hairdo and brown corduroys, my gender was indistinguishable from that of my brother and every other little boy in the neighborhood. I remember being mistaken for a boy fairly often. But androgyny had gone far out of fashion by the time my child was born. In 2011, it was nearly impossible to glance at a young child's clothing and guess their gender wrong. Unless, of course, you were looking at my son.

At playdates, all the moms complained about the resurgence in gendered toys and clothing, bemoaning the power wielded over their daughters by the Disney princesses, and rolling their eyes at their sons' obsessions with guns and race cars. But no one seemed to be fighting back all that hard. Even my staunchest feminist friends marveled helplessly at the power of nature. "It's just how it is," they'd shrug. "They seem to be wired that way."

I knew, of course, that there really wasn't such a thing as a girl color, or toy, or career. I had taken women's studies classes in college. I had a subscription to *Ms.* magazine. I knew that each generation's unquestioned assumptions about gender roles would be mocked and tossed aside by the next. Perhaps one day my grandchildren would buy dresses for their little boys or return to the androgynous days of bowl-cuts and brown corduroys, but I didn't have time to wait for social norms to evolve. I needed a world that would allow for a child like mine. Right now.

I decided to create one. I couldn't change all the toy stores and clothing aisles. I couldn't change the movies and TV ads. And I couldn't change the language spoken by the rest of the world.

But I *could* try to change the one we spoke. Inside our home, in our family, in our own little world, I decided, we would redefine gender—we would create a world in which boys could love pink and dream of princesses, and still be boys. We would expand the definition of "boy" to include my son.

I found a website selling pink T-shirts printed with the words BOYS CAN WEAR PINK, and I ordered one for my child, for his dad, and for his grandfathers. I sent the men an email explaining the important role they could play in defying society's narrow definitions of manhood. I included a link to a *Smithsonian* magazine article that explained how pink had been a "boy color" up until the 1940s because it was considered strong and decisive, while blue, being a daintier color, was deemed best for girls. "Let's reclaim pink for boys and men!" I wrote and asked them to consider wearing their new stereotype-smashing T-shirts when they spent time with my son.

---

A June 1918 article from the trade publication *Earnshaw's Infants' Department* said, "The generally accepted rule is pink for the boys, and blue for the girls. The reason is that pink, being a more decided and stronger color, is more suitable for the boy, while blue, which is more delicate and dainty, is prettier for the girl."

—*Smithsonian* magazine, April 7, 2011

---

I let my child sign up for the ballet classes he had been begging for and bought him a tutu and pale pink slippers over the objections of the horrified young woman at the dance supply store, who kept trying to tell me that "the *boys'* slippers are *black*" until I interrupted her to explain that "*my* boy loves pink!"

I smiled conspiratorially at my son. "Isn't that right, sweetie?" He smiled back and asked how many tutus I would buy for him.

At ballet class, all the other moms assumed he *was* a girl, and they admired my little ballerina's unusually short haircut until I corrected them, too, with a friendly scold. "Surely boys can love ballet and pretty things?"

I went online to search for images of men and boys wearing the kinds of beautiful feminine clothing my child loved. There were lots of drag queens, but what I wanted to find were photos of people who just looked like . . . regular guys, but who also just happened to be wearing dresses and frills. You can find lots of people like this online these days—beautiful bearded boys in pencil skirts and sundresses. But this was back in 2012, when no one had yet heard of Caitlyn Jenner, let alone a bathroom bill. Donald Trump was still hosting *The Apprentice*, and mainstream gender expression was still relentlessly traditional. All my searches came up empty.

Ultimately, and absurdly, I found myself combing through websites on European art, looking for historic portraits from eras when powerful men had been allowed to wear gorgeous things: Renaissance dandies in striped tights and ruffled shirts, eighteenth-century aristocrats sporting long, curled wigs and silken slippers, toes pointed daintily as dancers.

I lined up a gallery of images on my laptop and called my child to my side. "Look at these pretty clothes these men are wearing!"

I said, pulling him into my lap and pointing at the screen. "Those are MEN. In the past, all the men wanted to dress like this."

My four-year-old looked at his mother like I had just said the cat was going to cook dinner. But I was desperate. Somehow, I *had* to remake the world in my child's image. Somehow, I had to provide him an avenue to manhood.

"These are the kinds of pretty things *you* like, sweetheart!" I pointed at the golden tights of a powder-faced nobleman flanked by his pack of hunting dogs.

An image I showed my child

He dutifully leaned in and squinted at the picture on the screen. "I like that little brown doggie," he said, and wriggled off my lap.

One day another boy showed up in ballet class. I was thrilled. Unlike my boy, he was dressed like one, in gray sweats with white gym socks. Surrounded by diaphanous tutus and pink leotards, he looked like a dark bug in the middle of a bridal bouquet. And he looked miserable, sulking through the routines, phoning in his twirls, staring sullenly at the floor a few feet in front of him. I wondered why he had been forced to do something he so obviously hated. After class, I followed him to his mother. She was surprised when I told her there was another boy in the class. And then she looked down at my child and smiled grimly. "Oh. Caleb wants to wear that stuff, too, but we only let him do that at home."

The two little dancers looked each other over, clearly confused. The one in gray pointed at the one in pink and turned to me. "That's a *boy*?"

"Yes, Caleb, he's a boy," I said. "He's a boy who loves ballet, like you."

I expected my outgoing child to smile at his new friend, but instead he frowned and kicked the wall, crumpling the soft toe of his pale pink slipper. It looked painful. His lower lip popped out. Caleb's mom took his hand and pulled him away.

I hustled my own child out to our car, hoping he hadn't noticed the look on the woman's face. He was silent until we were buckled in. "It isn't nice when you do that, Mama." He glared at me in the rearview mirror.

"Do what?"

"When you tell people I'm a boy. It is *not* nice."

"But you *are* a boy, sweetheart," I said. It didn't seem fair not to say what was true. "You're a boy because you have a pen—"

"No," he interrupted me. "I'm never a boy."

I had no idea how to argue with this declaration. But I also wasn't prepared to agree with it, so I opted for a compromise. "OK," I said. "I'll stop telling people you're not a girl. Would that make you feel better?"

He snorted, rolling his eyes, as if to say, *If that's the best you can do, lady.*

For now, it was.

HELPFUL (AND CONCERNED) FRIENDS and relatives suggested I read him a popular new children's book called *My Princess Boy*. It's about a boy who loves princess stuff and whose family accepts him just as he is, dresses, sparkles, and all. I bought the book and ended up with several more copies of it, gifts from the same helpful and concerned friends and relatives. We read it exactly once. After the last page was turned, he slammed it shut and threw it across the room.

"I hate that book," he said.

"Why? Why do you hate it?"

"You know why, Mama," he said.

> **Me:** What are your favorite things to play with?
>
> **My child (age three):** My princess things.
>
> **Me:** Why do you like princesses so much?
>
> **My child:** I just kinda do.
>
> **Me:** Do you think it's OK for boys to like princesses?
>
> **My child:** But I'm a girl.

I LAY AWAKE IN BED every night as my brain did relentless and fruitless battle with the same questions. How in the world was I going to convince my little boy that he was one? And that he *wanted* to be one? How can someone not want to be what they are?

❖

I CALLED OUR PEDIATRICIAN and explained that my son wanted to be a girl. I told him about the sparkly clothes and fairies and potions that can melt off penises. After a few minutes, I wondered if our call had been cut off, because people don't usually listen so much and say so little.

"Are you still there?" I said.

The young doctor cleared his throat and said this was new territory for him, as if my child were an unexplored region of space. Was my child really such a rare phenomenon? Were we really this alone? He promised to do some research and call me back.

I hung up and felt appallingly insecure. What exactly had I told him? The words had tumbled out of me in a rush, crammed together and sped up, the way a guilty person speaks. I imagined him calling his colleagues to confer about where I'd gone wrong.

My sister said she knew another mom with a son who sounded kind of like mine. "I think he wore skirts to kindergarten," she said. When I met the mom for coffee, she told me that her seven-year-old son sometimes wore girl clothes but never claimed he actually *was* a girl. She pulled a book out of her purse and pushed it across the table at me. "You can keep it. I think you need it more than I do." I read the title and resisted the urge to push it right back to her. It was called, *The Transgender Child*.

To be polite, I thanked her and stuffed it in my purse, but I had no intention of reading it. I'd heard this word, *transgender*, and I knew enough to know it was represented by the *T*, which came right after the three gay letters, *L-G-B*, and nobody I knew was shocked by these letters anymore in my liberal West Coast city. My parents had even attended a lesbian wedding recently.

But no one spoke about the *T*. The *T* was something I wanted to squirm away from. I associated it with lurid movie plots involving prostitutes and trashy talk shows like Jerry Springer, where people slept with their girlfriends' mothers and threw chairs and pulled each other's hair while the crowd hooted and jeered at the train-wrecked lives on stage. What could any of that possibly have to do with my precious, innocent young child?

The pediatrician called back and said this wasn't really in his "wheelhouse," but he could refer us to a psychologist who specialized in this sort of thing.

According to her internet bio, the psychologist was an expert on kids and gender, who had trained at a prestigious East Coast children's hospital. I made an appointment right away. Then I asked my child, "Does your papa know that you want to be a girl?"

"Of course he does," he replied. Before we split, Will and I had agreed that our son might be gay, and that this would be OK. And apparently my ex had also come to terms with our son's princess-loving ways and feminine fashion choices. The Hello Kitty backpack that traveled with our son between our two homes was stuffed with tutus and sparkly headbands. But we had never spoken about the idea that perhaps we didn't actually have a son. Most of our handoffs involved one of us dropping off at preschool and the other one picking up, so we managed to avoid each other pretty effectively. I'd been hoping we would be on better terms by the time the issue needed to be dealt with—if ever.

But our child couldn't wait for his parents any longer.

I sat down and wrote Will an email. "Our child has told me numerous times that he isn't a boy," I wrote. "He even told me he wanted to go back in my womb and come back out again as a girl." I told him about the psychologist and suggested that he come with us to the appointment. "I have no idea where we are headed," I added. "But I think we need to get some help."

Will wrote back and said it couldn't hurt to get some advice and he'd meet me at the appointment. He said he wasn't too concerned about it, though, which simultaneously annoyed me and calmed me. Worrying had always been *my* job, not his.

THE PSYCHOLOGIST WAS YOUNG, efficient, and sympathetic. While our child played in another room with an assistant, Will and I took turns telling her why we were there. *He isn't like the other boys at all. He seems so incredibly drawn to "girl things." Do you think he might be gay? We just want him to be happy, whoever he is.*

Then she sent us out of the room so she could have a chat alone with our child. I noticed she had a lot of toys in her office. And art supplies. Would she ask him to draw a self-portrait? Pick out his favorite toys? Would this tell her his future? What would she see that we could not?

Then she brought us back in and told us the things that every cell in my body was crying out to hear. She pronounced our child psychologically healthy and happy. No red flags. And then she said, "Your child *could be* transgender, but the reality is that it's not very likely." She said studies had shown that 80 percent of children like ours ended up *not* being transgender.

Eighty percent.

Eighty was a big, comforting number. I asked her to repeat it. *Eighty percent. Eighty percent.* I whispered that statistic to myself as I drove home. I may have sung it quietly, too. In the weeks that followed, I repeated it, over and over and over, to family and friends, reassuring all of us that this "girl thing" was, in all likelihood, *statistically*, not going to last. *Eighty percent* not likely to last. I still had not cracked the cover of that frightening book, *The Transgender Child*, and now it seemed I probably wouldn't need to. That book was written for the statistically puny 20 percent—a small, sad slice of probability that I had no time for.

My crowd of helpful and concerned family and friends responded enthusiastically to the 80 percent news. I got the feeling they'd been eager for this opening to weigh in with supporting evidence. After my child spent a weekend with his grandparents, my dad reported that he and his best friend had watched his grandson carefully and had subsequently determined that he was "all boy." The two men spent their retirement doing guy stuff together—fixing lawn mowers and dynamiting old stumps. So I guessed they'd know a boy when they saw one.

My cousin agreed: "It's just how he moves, you know?" she said. "It's the way a *boy* moves." She had two kids, one of each. So maybe *she* really could discern one from the other. Others noted his love of swords and rough play. His physicality. His confidence. His independence. His persistence. My mom commented on his stoicism when injured. I ignored the egregiousness of this sexist stereotyping and took it all in like a sopping-wet animal, rescued from drowning, drying out in the sun. *At last.*

BUT THE FACT REMAINED that my child winced every time I used his name or referred to him with male pronouns. Each and every *he, him,* or *his* appeared to land on his body like darts, precise and painful, and I could not bear to be the one throwing them. If he really was "all boy," he certainly didn't know it yet.

I had already attempted to redraw the boundaries of boyhood to make room for him. And I had also stopped correcting people who thought he was a girl. The only option left seemed to be to eradicate gender entirely.

So began the period of our lives that I now think of as The Great Avoidance. Since my child couldn't bear to be called by a boy name, and I was not willing to call out a girl one, my child became essentially nameless. And I addressed this little person with a series of (mostly) gender-neutral endearments: Sweetheart, Kiddo, Love Bug, Pumpkin, and sometimes, per special request, Rainbow.

Pronouns were trickier. If I absolutely *had* to refer to my offspring in the third person, I performed feats of verbal gymnastics, developing a repertoire of genderless pronoun alternatives.

"Hi, Mom, glad you called. Yes, my kiddo is doing great. We just got home from the park and . . . your grandchild had a blast."

"Did he?" she replied, "Oh, right, I forgot you're doing the 'no gender' thing! What should I call him? Oh, dear, this *is* tricky. What should I call . . . my grandchild?"

I had no idea. I was inhabiting a lonely and awkward twilight, waiting for my 80-percent statistic to bear fruit. It was a relief to abandon the words that had made my child wince and crumple, but I also knew that this genderless no-man's-land wasn't sustainable.

Gender was out there, waiting for us.

STEP TWO

# *Let go.*

The school year was a few weeks underway. I had just kissed my child goodbye at morning drop-off when the preschool teacher asked me to join her in the craft room for a private chat. "He told us he's a girl and his name is M.," she said. "Our teaching staff is wondering how we should handle this, and we agreed I would speak with you." The teacher kept on talking. I heard the words *diversity* and *compassion* and also *controversial*, but I wasn't really following.

The teacher had said "M." M. is my younger sister's name. My child's beloved Aunt M. He had named himself after his aunt, my only sister, whose name is common and kind of old-fashioned and not the slightest bit fanciful. Nothing like Rainbow. This was not fairy magic, this was startlingly mundane. My child was laying claim to a spot among the ranks of the family's living, breathing women, and this shook me harder than every frilly, sparkly salvo he had lobbed my way up until this moment.

The teacher still seemed to be speaking. She said, "So, how about you talk this over with his dad and get back to me?"

That weekend there was an afternoon kids' rock concert at the local library. The lead guitarist was a dad my sister knew from her son's school. The all-dad band sang catchy, clever songs about things like macaroni and cheese, robots, and learning to tell time. My sister and I stood at the back with the other parents while my nephews sat among the cross-legged kids on the carpet in front of the small stage. My child had found a spot off to the side, where he stood and marched in place to the music, mesmerized, his gaze fixed on the lead singer. After the second song was done, he ran back to me and tugged on my hand. "I need to go on stage with them, Mama!"

I turned to my sister. "Do you think they'd mind?"

She shrugged. "Heck, why not?" She winked at her nephew. "You can at least ask."

When the next song finished, my child ran up to the stage. I watched the lead singer crouch down to talk to the small figure in the hot-pink party dress that I had recently been talked into buying. The tiny fan appeared to be making an expressive case, arms waving, head bobbing. The musician dad listened with a surprised smile. Then he turned to his bandmates, who grinned and nodded and beckoned their little fan to join them.

I watched as my child made his way to center stage, faced the audience, and began tapping the next song's beat with the toe of a sparkly pink tennis shoe. When the band began to sing, he closed his eyes, tilted back his head, and began belting out a song he had never heard before, his mouth opening and closing around words he alone could hear.

"Amazing," my sister said, as we both cracked up. "My nephew is amazing."

The song ended and the lead singer leaned into the mic. "Hey folks! Looks like we have a new member of our band! Do you

Joining the band, age four

want to introduce yourself?" He lowered his mic stand to half its height.

"Hi! I'm M.!" the tiny rock star shouted into the microphone.

Aunt M.'s eyes bulged. "Did he just say . . . ?"

"Yep."

"Wow. Just . . . wow."

◈

SITTING IN A CONFERENCE ROOM at the children's hospital, I was fighting back tears, and the fluorescent lights offered my grief no cover. The other parents at the Gender Diversity support group gave me sympathetic frowns and slid a box of tissues down the table toward me. I was telling them about the night, a few weeks ago, when my son had sobbed himself to sleep after learning that one day he was going to grow a beard like his dad. "How could a four-year-old care so much about something like that?" I said. "I mean, most little boys aren't scared of having beards, are they?"

The other parents shook their heads in confirmation. No, most little boys aren't scared of beards. I took a deep breath and told them the rest. How my son loved princesses and ballet, and how he loathed short haircuts, sports, and everything else associated with boys. How his face lit up when people mistook him for a girl. How for his fourth birthday, he asked for a poofy party dress and a vagina.

"I was able to give him just one of those," I joked, wanting to hear people laugh, and they obliged.

This evening was turning out to be strange and wonderful. Over the past several months, I had been sharing small parts of my story with friends and other parents at preschool. "He wants to be Tinker Bell for Halloween," I might tell a mom at a playdate. Or, "He says he has a girl heart." I watched the reactions race across their faces before they could hide them from me— shock, concern, disbelief. And then, usually, awkward silence. If they didn't change the subject or walk away, I rushed in with my explanations, my defense: *I'm as perplexed as you are! He's always just been like this. He's very close to his dad.*

After one too many of these lonely interactions, I realized I needed to find some people who didn't find my child so strange. Blessedly, tonight, I was finally among them. None of the support group parents seemed to expect any explanations. When I paused and glanced around the room, no one looked shocked. No one looked away. So I kept talking until I had told them about the November evening that had changed everything, when my son told me he wanted to go back in my womb to be born again as a girl.

"I think you're in the right place, Marlo," the support group leader said. He had a kind, youthful face and a neat gray beard, and there was recognition in his sparkling brown eyes. I hoped and expected him to say he had a kid just like mine, but instead he asked if anyone else wanted to share.

Over the next two hours, I heard from parents whose boys had become girls, and whose girls were now boys. And from those whose kids were staking out a spot somewhere in the middle, insisting they were neither one nor the other.

I also learned the term "social transition," which is what many of their kids had done, changing from one gender to another just by buying new clothes and changing names and pronouns. "It's pretty simple," a woman said. "We're not talking about kids having surgeries here. We just let our kid cut his hair and start shopping in the boys' section." She looked at me and smirked. "It sounds like your kid has already started their social transition."

Around the table, heads nodded knowingly. "He's only four years old!" I said, embarrassed to hear myself almost shouting. But this was all moving way too fast. And besides, what did these people know about my child? They had never laid eyes on him!

The smirking mom raised her eyebrows. "Did *you* know *your* gender at four?"

"Yes. Probably." I tried to remember. "But I was just a regular girl, so it never came up."

"Exactly. The kids who *aren't* trans get to know their gender, and proclaim it to the world, and no one questions it."

"But how do we *know* they're transgender and not just confused?" I said. "What if the real problem is that society places our kids into such narrowly defined gender boxes? Couldn't my son just be confused and think he's a girl because he likes lots of girl things?"

"That's a good point." The bearded facilitator chuckled. "It's a crazy, mixed-up world when it comes to gender, that's for sure."

The parents shook their heads and smiled. "So true, so true," they said.

But I wasn't smiling. I was annoyed and impatient to get to the bottom of this. I turned to the facilitator to demand some answers. "How can we be *sure* what gender our kids are? Where is the actual evidence?" I explained that I'd been online, doing research and looking for something solid and scientific. And I had read about studies of brain scans and hormone levels. "Are any of those accurate?" I asked. "How can we be sure that this is real?"

"I'm afraid there's no blood test for transgender," he said. We all laughed. Of course there wasn't.

"But I want one!" I yelled, and everyone laughed again.

Smirking Mom winked at me. "Join the club, Mama."

After the meeting a couple of parents gave me their phone numbers and said I could call them anytime. I had the horrible feeling I'd just been initiated into a club I was not yet prepared to join. I was furious and grateful.

When I got home, my house was dark and cold and too quiet. I sat on the couch with the lights off and missed my child. I missed every cell of him. Weekends when he was with his dad were always hard, but this night felt barely tolerable.

I picked up my phone and looked at the new phone numbers from the support group parents, these magicians who had delivered on the impossible, turning their daughters into *T. rexes*, transforming their sons into slices of toast. I wondered if I'd ever call them, if I'd ever be one of them. The phone rang and it was Mom, calling to ask how the meeting had gone. I told her about social transition.

"So, there's nothing medical involved?" she asked. "No surgeries or drugs?"

"No, nothing."

"Well, that's a relief, isn't it?"

I told her about the children who were strewn around the hospital cafeteria outside the conference room when I arrived, playing board games and drawing pictures. A handful of attentive adults sat with them, rolling dice and admiring their colorful drawings. "They have free childcare for the kids," I explained, "so the parents can talk without being interrupted."

"Oh, that's wonderful!" she said, "Are they all . . . like my grandson?"

"I don't know. Probably."

I thought of a child I had noticed when I first arrived, playing a game with some other children. The child appeared to be a few years older than mine, maybe seven or eight, with very short hair and a Laura Ingalls–style pioneer girl dress, a size or two too large, over blue jeans and a long-sleeved white T-shirt. I imagined the dress being pulled on hastily in the car on the way there, or out in the hospital parking lot. Atop the regular clothes, it looked like dress-up. Except the child was not playing make-believe. The child was just playing, just being.

"Are you going to bring my grandson next time?" Mom asked.

"I don't know."

"You're doing a good job, honey."

"I have no idea what I'm doing."

I emailed Will and told him about the support group. I said I had found it "interesting and helpful" and gave him details for the next meeting. Then I crawled into bed with the book I had spent months not reading: *The Transgender Child: A Handbook for Families and Professionals* by Stephanie Brill and Rachel Pepper.

"There is a reason you have picked up this book," it began ominously. Then it told me many things I didn't want to know but badly needed to: Gender identity appears to be hardwired from birth. People seem to be "born this way," and it isn't caused by something the parents did wrong—like getting a divorce (thank God). Gender identity isn't the same thing as sexuality, though people confuse these two things all the time. (Gender identity is about who you *are*, not whom you will love.) And even though it seemed insane to take a four-year-old boy seriously when he said he was a girl, it actually wasn't. As the book's authors wrote: "Because gender identity emerges around the same time as a child learns to speak, it is common for children who are transgender to try to let their parents know this when they are very, very young." I reread this sentence several times, committing it to memory. If this kept up, I would need it for my defense.

However, the book went on to say that most kids are *not* transgender, even those who exhibit strong cross-gender behavior and interests. There were also no reliable data about how many of these children exist nor any definitive explanation behind *why* they exist. Like the support group leader had said, there was no blood test for transgender.

But there was a checklist. The book's checklist had been cre-ated by Dr. Norman Spack, cofounder of the GeMS clinic at Bos-ton Children's Hospital, the first clinic in the United States to treat transgender children. The checklist contained what Spack had witnessed in his extensive practice to be "reliable markers for a transgender identity."

It had just four items.

First was "bathroom behavior." If your son insists on peeing sitting down, or your daughter always stands up, that's a clue. The second was swimsuit aversion. The child refuses to wear a bathing suit that matches their anatomical sex. Third: the same thing, but for underpants. And finally, "A strong desire to play with toys typically assigned to the opposite sex."

I got out of bed and poured myself a glass of wine. *There is a reason you have picked up this book.* I thought of his little legs dangling against the edge of the toilet while he sat to pee, of the skirted swimsuit printed with strawberries he had worn all summer, of the package of Disney princess underpants I had just been talked into buying, of our houseful of fabulously pretty toys. I finished my wine and crawled back into bed and lay in the dark contemplating all the things I had not wanted to learn.

Among them was the fact that my "80 percent" statistic didn't hold up. According to the book's foreword, written by Dr. Nor-man Spack himself, the studies claiming that less than 20 per-cent of children like mine would end up transgender were riddled with flaws. I felt a door closing that might soon be shut tight, locked for good.

## The Perniciously Persistent "80 Percent" Myth

As a child psychologist said to me back in 2012, studies show that "more than 80 percent" of kids like mine will ultimately revert to living in the gender assigned to them at birth. I've been hearing this statistic ever since, and it perplexes me to no end, because I have never seen it reflected in reality. Over the past decade, I have encountered hundreds of parents like me, with children like mine: children who tell us, over an extended period of time, that they are not the gender we thought they were. And in all these years, I have never encountered a child like mine who took it all back. Not once. Perhaps this is for the same reason that I have never encountered a cisgender child who was truly secure and happy in their gender and who then suddenly proclaimed themselves to be another gender. Perhaps, in the case of both transgender kids and cisgender kids, we generally *do* know who we are from a very young age.

So why don't the studies back this up? As it turns out, the "science" underpinning the "80 percent" statistic is seriously flawed. Most of the studies behind the "80 percent" statistic were published more than thirty years ago and were based on data collected even earlier—in the 1950s, 1960s, and 1970s. None of these studies looked specifically at transgender kids (children who had *declared themselves to be another gender*). Instead, these studies included a range of children who were exhibiting behavior that deviated from the narrowly defined gender norms of the day (e.g., "effeminate" boys who liked dolls, or "tomboy" girls who hated wearing dresses). It does not surprise me that most of these kids grew up to be cisgender (though some of them did later identify as gay). As psychologist Dr. Kristina Olson wrote in an op-ed in 2016, critiquing the problematic studies behind the "80 percent" statistic, the evidence suggests that "most children in these samples were never transgender to begin with."[1] She went on to point out that we simply do not know how many transgender children will grow up to be transgender adults "because no long-term studies have recruited a large number of children who believe that they are members of the opposite sex nor separated the few they have included in past studies from the broader group of gender nonconforming children."

Dr. Olson's groundbreaking study, the TransYouth Project, aims to eventually answer this question, but it will take time. For now, the most reliable data we have are the reports from the medical professionals who have devoted their careers to working with these children. In 2017, the Gender Service at the Royal Children's Hospital in Melbourne, Australia, reported that 96 percent of all patients diagnosed with gender dysphoria between 2003 and 2017 continued to identify as transgender or gender diverse into late adolescence.[2] Dr. Daniel Metzger, a pediatric endocrinologist working with trans youth at BC Children's Hospital in Vancouver, Canada, reports similar numbers in his medical practice. As he told me, "We have seen nothing close to 80 percent desistance among prepubertal kids who insistently, persistently, and consistently say they are not the gender assigned to them at birth, once they reach puberty. Once children reach puberty, the desistance rate appears to be less than 1 percent."

SPRING SLIPPED BY. The days got longer and lighter, and my child's hair now covered his ears completely, bending awkwardly around them like golden earmuffs and reminding me of my own childhood bowl-cut hairdos. He said that the fairies must be getting tired of sleeping in the dirt, so he built them little houses out of sticks, with soft beds of moss.

He performed in his first ballet recital. I watched him skip and twirl with the same adorable clumsy abandon as the other tiny ballerinas and felt proud and scared. Caleb, the sad boy in gray, had dropped out of class.

A coworker told me the reason my child wanted to be a girl must be because I'd given him such a weird first name. My father offered to take his grandson to a baseball game. I avoided pronouns and the preschool teacher.

Sometimes, I tested the waters. "Who knows?" I said, in a daring mood at another preschooler's birthday party. "Maybe he'll go to kindergarten as a girl!"

"I don't think that's right," a mom said, and the room went quiet until someone suggested we serve the cake.

I kept on going to the support group, where I heard of astonishing things: a little girl who drew penises all over her bedroom walls with a Sharpie. A six-year-old boy who tried to jump off the roof of his house, hoping that in heaven he might finally be a girl. Another caught in the nick of time with a pair of scissors in the bathroom, attempting to fix God's mistake.

Children who stopped laughing, smiling, speaking; whose inexplicable anxieties and persistent self-negations terrified their parents and stumped their doctors; who scratched their heads and heaped another diagnosis atop their young shoulders, prescribed a different pill.

But in case after case, the skies did not clear until the adults in charge took one simple and gigantic step: They told their children that they could be who they said they were. And then, silent children spoke again. Anxious children grew calm. Sad children smiled. It sounded a lot like magic.

It was at the support group that I learned a new statistic: 40 percent. The suicide attempt rate for kids like mine is around 40 percent.* And those are the kids we know about, who have told someone that this is why they wanted to die.

Forty percent was a very high number. I didn't share this number with family and friends. Instead, I argued with it. *My* child was happy, or seemed to be. I tried to watch more closely. *Was* he growing sadder, more silent? Would he, like these other children, begin to find ways to disappear, to alter or erase himself?

I realized that he had stopped correcting me when I neglected my vow to banish gender and slipped back into sentences laced with *he*s and *him*s, or when I called out his boy name. Was it just my imagination, or did his little chest collapse and shoulders droop ever so slightly, when my mom referred to her "three

---

* Forty percent may, unfortunately, be a low estimate of the number of transgender youth attempting suicide. In a 2019 study published in the journal *Pediatrics*, more than half of transgender adolescents studied reporting having attempted suicide.[3]

beautiful grandsons"? Were these the first clues that my child was slowly slipping away from me, or was this all just a phase that would pass in time?

And what if—*what if*—we did take the plunge and got it wrong?

I tried to imagine how this might play out: We change genders, we tell everyone he's a girl, and then . . . he wants to switch back and be a boy. What then? Surely such a disaster would leave a lasting mark.

At the next support group, I lobbed this conundrum to the facilitator. It was all well and good to support our kids, I said, but shouldn't we tread cautiously? "What if these kids change their minds?"

He tilted his head and smiled at me, coyly. "Would that be so bad?"

This man was infuriating. "Well, wouldn't that be hard?" I demanded. "Not to mention confusing?"

"Hard and confusing for whom?"

What was wrong with this guy? Wasn't this obvious? "For him," I said. "For everyone."

And then the facilitator took a deep breath and said something like this: "OK. So, let's say you follow your kid's lead and they transition socially, or whatever it is they say they need to do with regard to their gender. What message would you be sending your child? *I* think the message would be this: that you believe them and support them, that you have their back, that you're with them on this journey, confusion and all, wherever it ends up. Whether they stay in that gender or they 'change back,' you'd have a child who was supported while they explored this gender thing and figured it out *with* you, instead of in spite of you. At the end of the day, I don't think that's going to be confusing. Not for your child. Maybe for the grandparents or the neighbors, but they'll get over it."

He was absolutely, exasperatingly right.

"Dammit," I said, "why can't he just be gay?"

"Yeah, we all say that," muttered the dad sitting next to me.

The facilitator folded his hands and looked me in the eyes. "Well, I'm transgender, and I feel pretty good."

"Oh, God, I'm sorry. I didn't mean—"

He held up a hand to stop me. "It's OK. This isn't easy stuff. Believe me, I know. What matters is that you're all *here*. You're here for your kids."

But was I?


THE PRESCHOOL TEACHER wanted to have another chat in the craft room. Apparently my kiddo had continued to take charge of things, informing everyone at school that he was now a girl whose name was M. "And his dad told us that they're using the name M. at his house now." She wanted to know if I was on board with this new name, so they could talk about next steps at school.

The room seemed to be tilting dangerously to the left. I lowered myself down into a tiny plastic chair to get it to stop, focusing my attention on a basket of glue sticks on the table in front of me. I heard the teacher say that this was going to be "tricky," and that the school would have to consider the other parents' feelings.

"We need to respect different families' belief systems," she said.

*Belief systems?*

The room abruptly righted itself. I felt a sudden urge to pick up the basket of glue sticks and throw it at her head. I heard myself ask: "Would we consider their 'belief systems' if they were racist?"

"That's not the same thing," she said.

"I think it is."

*Was* it the same? Not exactly, of course. I hadn't thought this through. I actually hadn't thought about it at all until this very moment. I had been completely preoccupied with my own responses to my child's battle with boyhood and hadn't spent much time considering how the wider world would respond to it. But they would be responding, of course. And what the preschool teacher was trying to tell me was that the response was going to include things I wasn't used to: Suspicion. Fear. Possibly rejection and exclusion. Because my child was different. And in that way, this *was* very much like racism and every other bigotry that hides behind euphemisms like "belief systems."

On the other hand, the teacher was correct in claiming that our situation *was* different from racism in many ways, and one of the ways was this: Although the other parents could be expected to have some idea about what racism was (and that it was bad), they probably couldn't be expected to know anything about transgender people, let alone transgender children. Nor could we assume that they would have any idea what transphobia was (and that it was also bad). If I'm being honest, I didn't have a clear handle on this myself. But what I heard the preschool teacher saying, loud and clear, was this: Your child's difference is a problem.

A mama-bear rage roared in my ears. Whoever my baby turned out to be, it would not be determined by community debate. "Well," I huffed, "*I* think the other parents at this school have some learning to do."

I tried to look dignified as I hauled myself out of the tiny plastic chair, then fled out to my car where I sat in the parking lot for a very long time, my indignation slowly giving way to rising panic. Were we really going to be rejected by the other parents at the school if my boy became a girl?

And what else was it that the teacher had said? Will had already let my child change genders at his house without telling me. *Without telling me?* How could he have taken such a life-altering step without consulting me first? Surely you have to consult the *mother* before you sign off on changing a young child's name. Or changing a young child's *gender.*

What in the world was my ex-husband thinking? Was he trying to undermine me, to score a victory in our silent, simmering war? Or did he assume I had already given in to our child, too, and made the switch? Or was he simply doing a better job than I was, listening to and supporting our child while I stalled and resisted, with my endless campaign of history lessons and feminist theory lectures and clever contortions of grammar? Had my child given up on me and turned to the parent who was actually willing to listen?

I remembered something a mom had said in a support group: "Our kids are already leaving the station. Are we gonna get on the train with them or get left behind?" I imagined all the other parents from preschool, whose "belief systems" must be "considered," standing on the platform with me, some tutting and shaking their heads, others deep in earnest discussion, while the train began to slide by us, picking up speed. We were all about to miss the train—but only *my* child was on it.

CLEARLY, I NEEDED MORE HELP. I got the name of a therapist who specialized in gender issues and booked an appointment with her for the following week. I figured I'd go alone first, to check her out, then bring my child to get him sorted out one way or another. I called up our insurance company to find out how many mental health visits our plan would cover for him.

"Twelve," the woman on the phone told me. "After you meet your deductible, and with a twenty-dollar co-pay. Hang on, let me just read you the exclusions." She droned through a list of verbal fine print. "Experimental therapies, nicotine-related disorders, academic or career counseling, marriage counseling, gender dysphoria, wilderness therapy . . ."

I interrupted her. "Sorry, could you repeat that last one?"

"Wilderness therapy?"

"No. I think you said 'gender' something?"

"Yes, um, it says 'mental health services not covered for gender dysphoria or issues related to sexual reassignment or gender change.' That one?"

I felt like I'd just stepped on a rake. "Yes, that one."

I thanked her and hung up. Maybe the therapist offered a sliding scale?

She did, but she said we could probably bill the visits under something related—like anxiety, perhaps.

"I don't think my kiddo is anxious, actually. He seems pretty happy, unless someone calls him a boy." I told her how much fun he seemed to be having in preschool. How he had lots of friends. How he seemed to be adjusting easily to dividing his time between his dad's house and mine.

It did sound like my child was doing well, she agreed. "But maybe someone else is anxious?"

My eyes filled with tears. "I'm just so scared, you know? It's so much to process."

She suggested I come back again the following week—on my own. I did. And the week after that. I sat on her couch and aired every last worry and doubt I could name and tried to get her to tell me what to do.

*Did she think this might all just be a phase? Was I overlooking something? What if I still needed to try one last thing that I hadn't yet tried? And was it OK if I just waited a bit longer and saw how things played out?*

She sat patiently through my questions. And my complaints. She listened for hours as I whined about the fact that there was no blood test, no brain scan, no psychologist who could ever give me a definitive diagnosis. And even if they could, no insurance would cover the treatment. None of my friends had a child anything like mine. None of the standard parenting books mentioned anything like this. And the collective wisdom of my family's matriarchy likewise came up empty; my mother and aunts and my ninety-nine-year-old grandmother were as perplexed by my child as I was.

"So it's all up to me," I declared, awash in self-pity. "I'm his mother. I have to say yes or no, boy or girl, like I'm God." It was too much, this awful burdensome power.

If I continued to push back, would my child one day try to jump off our roof? And if I said yes to girlhood, was I dooming my child to a life of perpetual pain and outsiderhood? Which choice held the greater dangers? "I don't want this choice," I said to my therapist. "I just can't make it."

"Well, that's great!" she replied. "Congratulations." She was actually smiling.

"What?"

"That you don't want this choice, this power to choose. Because you don't have it."

"I don't?"

"Nope."

Then she set me free.

"You know," she said, "if your child *isn't* transgender, there is nothing you can do to make them transgender. And if your child *is* transgender, there is nothing you do can do to stop them from being who they are."

She must have been saving this up for weeks, waiting for me to be ready to hear it. I wasn't in charge of this after all. I wasn't going to get to decide who my child was. *And*, I didn't have to. I did not possess this awful power. We parents do not get to decide who our children will be, at four or fourteen or forty. This fact is terrifying, but true.

"I'm going to go home and ask just one more time," I announced. "And whatever I hear, that's it. That will be it."

"Good luck."

THAT EVENING I INVITED MY CHILD to sit down on the living room couch. I sat down, too, at a polite distance, a couple of cushions away, as if my four-year-old were a barely acquainted guest and we were making awkward small talk before dinner. This oddness was noted. My little guest, perched at cushion's edge with legs dangling, watched me closely, attentive and still.

"I need to ask you a question," I said.

"What question, Mama?"

"Are you *really* sure that you want to be a girl?"

"No."

"No?" What the hell was this? Had I read everything wrong?

"I don't *want* to be a girl," my child said. "I *am* a girl."

And from that moment on, she was.

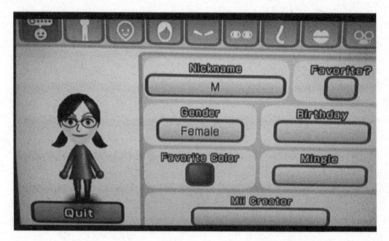

My daughter's Wii avatar

# Tell your story.

**"I** guess you probably need some more girl clothes," I said.

"Lots more," she said. So we went shopping, like mothers and daughters do, in the aisles full of the pretty things she had always wanted. And for the first time, my shoulders didn't tense, my mind didn't race, silently begging my child: *Please don't want that, please don't ask for that.*

In the fitting room, I watched her twirl in front of the mirror, delighting in her fabulous reflection.

"Can I have this one, too?"

Yes.

"And this one in both colors?"

Yes.

This day, I got to say yes, and only yes. We bought far more than one little girl needed, plus a tiara and a sparkly purse and rainbow hair clips. She squealed and threw her skinny arms around my hips. "Thank you, Mama! Thank you thank you thank you!!"

The scale of her delight broke my heart. I thought back to the dismal scene in our living room the previous Christmas morning, when she had opened the last of her gifts. It had been my final attempt at shopping for a son—dinosaur figurines, a robot, building kits of various kinds. My child had scanned the objects strewn around the living room, perplexed, and asked, "Didn't Santa get my letter?"

I threw a sparkly fairy wand in our shopping cart. Christmas was coming in May this year. It was remarkable, after so much angst, so much hand-wringing and second-guessing, how relatively simple and smooth it was, gaining a daughter. It was as if she had always been there, and I guess she had, waiting for me to see her. Waiting for me to say yes. She shrugged off boyhood like a scratchy sweater and plunged into girlhood without looking back.

But my worries weren't gone, they were just joined by new ones: Would she have a good life? How would the world respond to us? And what would happen when she hit puberty? Was I *really* doing the right thing?

Her joy was my beacon. My disappointed and frustrated child had been replaced by a deliriously happy one. What parent wouldn't make that trade? A tension drained from our days, the invisible battles over names, clothes, colors . . . gone, in one fell swoop. She was at peace, and so were we.

My fight with my child was finally over. And my fight with the rest of the world began.

❖

---

### American Psychological Association

### FACT SHEET: Gender Diversity and Transgender Identity in Children[4]

Gender identity development occurs much earlier than the development of sexual orientation. Children usually have a sense of their gender identity between age two to five and they typically become cognizant of their sexual orientation around age nine or ten, although this self-awareness is occurring at earlier ages, particularly as it is a topic more widely discussed and available to younger children. Transgender and gender diverse children may begin to play in a way that is not expected for children of their sex from a very young age. Gender diverse boys typically experience more negative reactions from their parents and experience more victimization at school than gender diverse girls. This is due to the great latitude given to girls expressing masculine behaviors in a society that overvalues male behaviors and undervalues female behaviors.

---

"YOUR FATHER WANTS TO TALK with you," Mom said to me. Then she whisper-shouted into the phone: "He doesn't really get it, honey!"

Fortunately, my father is a very kind man. "Now, please help me understand this." His tone was tender and tentative, like when he asked about my love life since my divorce. "Is this the same as gay?"

"No. This has nothing to do with sex, Dad. Transgender is who you *are*, not whom you love. Little kids aren't old enough to really know who they're attracted to. But they do know what gender they are, right?"

"Ah, yes, I see. So, is my grandchild gay?" Dad was going to take some time.

Mom, on the other hand, didn't miss a beat. She actually seemed excited. "I always wanted a granddaughter," she said. "Now I finally have one!" She asked when she could take her new granddaughter shopping.

When I told my ninety-nine-year-old grandmother that her youngest great-grandchild was now a girl, she shrugged, unimpressed. "Oh, we *always* knew there were people like that. A lot of them were hairdressers, you know. Or in the theater." Her face turned sad, perhaps remembering someone. "It was so hard for them."

A gay hairdresser wasn't exactly the same thing, but it was close enough for me. I waited for her to ask the questions everyone else was asking: *Was I sure? Shouldn't we wait?* She was nearly a century old and had nine great-grandchildren, so maybe she knew better than to fight these things. She just patted my hand and said, "We are who we are, dear. We are who we are."

The family matriarchs turned out to be outliers. Mom told me that my dad and brother-in-law were saying I just needed to make my child wear some pants. "Now, don't you worry," she said. "Men are kind of slow sometimes." But it wasn't just the men. Everyone listened kindly, but I could tell they weren't really buying it. I knew they just weren't sold on this transgender thing.

My sister said it was really hard for her kids to accept no longer having a male cousin, and she didn't want to push them. Some relatives said my child was not a girl at all, just spoiled, as if becoming a girl was like getting a pony. One friend pointed out that my child had always been awfully headstrong and "controlling," as if changing genders was just a convenient excuse to boss everyone around.

And *everyone* complained that they just couldn't get used to the different pronouns. I knew it was tricky—I struggled with it myself. At first, it felt clumsy and forced, like writing with the wrong hand. And for a while my brain's pronoun center seemed to be temporarily scrambled, and I got *everyone's* pronouns wrong—my best friend, my dog, the president. But I kept trying, waiting for my brain to believe me and make the switch. Because my child needed me to. I saw how much it hurt her when I got it wrong. I don't think anyone else really understood that yet. Instead, I got the feeling that they were all waiting for this girl thing to blow over.

"*She*, not *he*," I said, over and over and over. "I think you meant to say *her*."

"Oh, right. Sure. Sorry. I forgot. It's so *hard* for me to remember!"

No one objected for religious or moral reasons. My family went to church sometimes, but none of us were particularly religious, nor were any of my friends. I knew they weren't being deliberately cruel. They just found it . . . weird. And I couldn't blame them. This *was* really weird.

I felt like that character at the beginning of a movie who is the sole witness to the landing of an alien spacecraft or the appearance of a mythical creature. She is wild-eyed with excitement and desperate to share her discovery, but she ends up just sounding crazy: "I *know* it sounds crazy!" she says, "but I *promise* you, it's real! Hear me out: It's a child with the body parts of a boy but who actually *is* a girl. Or, it could also be a girl who's actually a boy!"

The other characters in the movie are skeptical, to say the least. If such creatures actually exist, why hadn't *they* ever encountered one themselves? "But you have!" she insists. "They're all around us! At your office, in your neighborhood, in your own family!" Which is totally crazy. So of course, no one believes her. But they do worry about her. She seems so worked up.

And I was. Nobody seemed to understand how momentous this story was, and that there really was a unicorn in the garden, a spaceship crashed in the cornfield.

Well, actually, there *was* one other person who had seen these wonders. But we still weren't really talking. I know it sounds insane, immature, and wildly irresponsible, that our child had changed genders and we hadn't spoken about it. I felt a little better when someone told me that you *need* to get really angry when you break up after so many years together. How else can you cope with losing the person who used to be your everything? Hate hides the heartbreak.

So, Will and I fumed in our separate silos for a very long time, barely communicating. And somehow, it was OK. By some miracle we both arrived at the same place at around the same time. I see now that that miracle was just four years old.

M. APPARENTLY USED the same relentless tactics at preschool that she had used on her parents, because by the time I wrapped my head around having a daughter and approached her teacher to let her know, it was already a settled matter. "She kind of took care of it herself," the teacher said. "She told all the other kids and they're calling her M. now." The other kids really seemed fine with it, she said, "for the most part."

And the other part? "If they use the old name, she corrects them right away." I braced myself

> **Me:** Do you have any advice for kids who are transgender?
>
> **M. (age six):** Well, if somebody keeps saying, "No, you're a boy" or "No, you're a girl," don't give up. Just keep on convincing them. And get a grown-up if they tease you. You don't give up on being transgender. So, if people think you're a boy, and you're trying to convince them that you're a girl, you can't just give up and say, "Well, I'm a boy who likes pink and purple." It can be other ways. Don't give up. Not at all.

for her to bring up the other parents' "belief systems" again, but she didn't. She just asked if I wanted to make some kind of official announcement to the school community. An email to her classmates' parents? Something in the school newsletter?

I had heard about letters like this at the support group, circulated among friends, family, churches and schools, painstakingly crafted by parents like me, to gently convince, cajole, and instruct, and to draw our new lines in the sand: This is now the name, this is the pronoun.

I tried to imagine all the conversations a letter like this might lead to, once I'd made public an assertion I would have to defend. And I did not have any guarantee about whose side the school might take if another family objected. "How about we just wait and see how things go?" I said.

❖

THE WEATHER WAS CLEAR and pleasant, and I was afraid. I stood on my front porch, looking up and down the block, considering the best approach. I'd been putting this off for a few weeks, but my daughter was with her dad for the weekend, and I needed to do this without her, so it was time. Several of my neighbors were outside working in their front yards. A family strolled down the sidewalk, the dad wearing a baby on his chest while the mother hovered over a toddler on a tricycle. I heard kids shouting from someone's backyard.

We lived on a city block of small, square houses mostly filled with middle-aged couples and young families. I was friendly with a few of them, and I knew the names of most of the kids and dogs, but at least half of them were a mystery to me. I would skip those. The ones who needed to know were the ones who remembered the day I had brought home my baby boy from the hospital and who had greeted my child by name when he scampered up the sidewalk in his increasingly pretty clothing: The preteen girl two doors up who taught him how to do cartwheels on the front lawn, and whom he idolized. The collection of little kids at the end of the street who called out his now-defunct name when we passed by on our walk to the park.

I took a steadying breath and marched myself out to the sidewalk, feeling the invisible but mighty weight of what I carried before me and would soon offer up to strangers, door-to-door, like a nervous salesman: a platter with my heart on it. This was to be the first group of people I would tell who were under no prior obligation to love us—or interact with us ever again, if they so chose. Family and close friends had not worried me much; whether they agreed with me or not, I knew we probably wouldn't lose them.

But these powerful strangers could shut the door on us, and they would be in our lives for years to come, waving from their driveways in the morning, trick-or-treating at my doorstep, exchanging pleasantries in the grocery store checkout line, swapping neighborhood news and tips on the local schools. Or not.

This day is now a blur. I remember saying the same things, over and over, to unsuspecting neighbors who were out weeding their flower beds or surprised to find me on their front porches. What was I selling?

*You know how my kiddo always wears pink and dresses, like a girl? Well . . .*

*So the new name is M. And she really gets upset if you use her old name.*

*Could you please explain this to your kids?*

I was breathless and overeager, like the rookie I was, leaving little space for them to absorb, let alone comment. Would they buy it? Or would they shut the door on my face?

The response was uniformly calm and kind, but inscrutable to me. Perhaps if I lived in another part of the country, my neighbors would have laid their cards out for me to see. But my city in the Northwest is famous for its polite reserve. Newcomers find this infuriating, and lifelong residents like myself get used to not quite knowing where we stand.

I went home and collapsed on the couch, overwhelmed by the thought of how many more of these conversations lay ahead. There were so many people to tell, in so many spheres of our lives. But it turned out that information this interesting spreads quickly. Around my office. Among the extended family. Staff I barely knew at the preschool began giving me and my daughter knowing looks. And the neighbors who knew filled in those who did not. Gossip performed its age-old function, and the word was soon out: My son was now my daughter.

# Prepare.

W e were inching our way across the city, and when I pulled up to yet another stoplight, the child in the back seat said she was bored and wanted to go home.

I tried to drum up enthusiasm about where we were going. "Most of the kids there will be girls with penises, and boys with vaginas!" I had not yet taught her the word *transgender*. I thought it had too many syllables and too little meaning for a four-year-old. "Girl with a penis," on the other hand, was concrete and descriptive, devoid of adult mysteries. "You get to hang out with a bunch of kids like you. Isn't that cool?"

She looked out the car window and considered. "The art was fun last time. Can I do art again today?"

"I'm sure you can, yes! And while you make art, I'll be right next door in a room talking to the other parents about . . . how we can support you and understand you and . . . ways to help you."

"The *whole* time?"

"Uhh, yes."

Yes, I am driving across the city to sit in a stuffy room for two hours and talk with other parents about the fact that you have a penis. So much for dispelling mystery.

She shook her head at the bizarre behavior of adults. "I think art is more fun."

We arrived, and I left her to glue and scribble, looking happy and unconcerned, and went into the room next door to learn how to keep her that way. There was a new family that afternoon. There was a new one every time, it seemed, and I was starting to see the rhythm of it: usually a couple, the strain on them—perhaps between them—palpable. Often one of them, usually the dad, clearly doesn't want to be there and was likely dragged along. They are incredulous, frightened, sometimes angry, and there are always tears—so many tears, which they invariably apologize for.

And they tell us their remarkably familiar stories, still believing theirs is unique to them, as the rest of us nod and pass them tissues and wait for them to get it all out. Little "boys" who fashioned long hair out of anything, everything: a pair of pants, a towel, an older sister's tights. Little "girls" who stuffed socks down their pants, who shaved their own heads with their dad's electric razor. Children who say they wish they had never been born. Or who want a do-over, like mine did. Or who beg to stay small forever so they won't have to choose one gender or the other, because both options feel equally wrong, equally intolerable.

Families began to appear from other states. Like refugees, they had left behind jobs, lifelong friendships, grandparents, entire extended families, in search of safety, in search of a place where their child's life might be viable. It was from them that I learned how fortunate I was, and how rare this was. I happened to live in one of the handful of US states with any legal protection at all for transgender people, let alone community support or resources like this group. The gender refugees told us how their family businesses had been boycotted, their longtime friends no longer answering their calls, the doors of their churches shut to them, their kids ejected from schools and banned from play-groups, and death threats—against them and their *children*—left on their voicemail.

But not all the horror stories were imported across state lines. "Kids here are excluded and bullied, too," the local parents warned. "And the worst bullies are often the other parents. Or the teachers." One child's tormentor had been the school nurse. A shudder went around the room. No one was jaded about a child being hurt.

The facilitator told us that he was busy traveling across the state and to other states, trying to teach people about our children. "I'm afraid lots of people—maybe most people—think this is crazy, what we're doing here," he said. At conferences, at schools, in boardrooms, he was trying to explain our plight to the experts—to the doctors, the psychologists, the educators, the lawmakers. "But most of them still don't believe your kids really exist."

"No kidding. This hospital won't even treat our kids," a woman muttered. "Can you believe that?"

"You are pioneers," the facilitator went on. "All of you are pioneers. And revolutionaries. You and your kids are changing the world."

It did feel revolutionary. And daunting and disconcerting. In this sterile hospital conference room, while our kids played Candy Land and glued glitter onto popsicle sticks next door, we plotted our parental rebellion, strategizing ways to peacefully upend a centuries-old system, and in the meantime, we swapped hard-won recon on how to help our kids survive in hostile territory.

We learned how to recruit allies from among the long list of potential foes: school principals, sports coaches, doctors, ex-spouses, in-laws. How to prepare your child for the bullies (role-playing, *lots* of role-playing). How to navigate the multitude of minefields presented by sleepovers, swimming parties, locker rooms, and bathrooms, bathrooms, bathrooms.

"Everyone is obsessed with bathrooms," the facilitator warned. "When I do presentations at schools, that's all they want to talk about. As if your children go in there to do anything other than use the toilet!"

We learned where you could go for medical care: Boston had a Children's Hospital that would help. You could get a top-quality vagina in Bangkok if your child was over eighteen. Prior to that, the key word was "blockers": medications that pressed the "pause" button on puberty, so you could buy time.

We learned how to update your child's legal documents to erase old names and gender markers. And how to dress for success: For trans girls like mine, it was all about layers, and skirts were your best friend—worn over leggings, sewn onto swimsuits. For boys, one of our moms would modify their underpants for you, sewing a soft bulge into the crotch.

And we learned how to handle schools: Assume that *all* the parents will talk, and that the principal hates it when you rock the boat. If it gets too bad, switch schools and tell no one. And if all else fails, move. Start over fresh someplace new.

"And safe folders," the woman next to me said. "We really should *all* have a safe folder."

"Yes," the facilitator said. "Everyone know what a safe folder is? Cathy, why don't you explain?" Cathy had been at almost all the meetings since I started coming. And she'd been there at the group's inception, four years earlier, which made her a respected veteran. Her transgender daughter sounded like a slightly older version of mine.

Cathy explained that a "safe folder" was a collection of documents we should all gather and keep readily accessible at home: a doctor's letter confirming your child's diagnosis, and the same from a psychologist, for backup. Letters attesting to your parenting abilities, written by reputable people in your life: work colleagues, your child's teachers, your church pastor. Photos of your child exhibiting unconventional gender expression from a young age. "It's a good idea to include art, too," Cathy said. "Self-portraits they've drawn of themselves in their true gender."

"But why? What's it for?" someone asked.

"In case CPS knocks on your door," Cathy said. "Child Protective Services. If someone calls them and reports anything, they are required by law to investigate. The neighbors could report you, or some acquaintance. It could be anyone. It happens. Even here."

"But can they *actually* take away our kids for this?" I asked.

Cathy was silent. We turned to the facilitator.

"It's best to be prepared," he said. "Just in case."

The two hours were up, and we filed out of the room to reclaim our children. Mine skipped up to me and thrust a drawing into my hands: "A present. I drew it for you." It was of a girl with long golden hair reaching almost to her feet, a purple triangle for a dress. Above her floated a flock of yellow butterflies, each attached to a string, which the girl held gathered in one hand, like balloons, or a flying bouquet.

"It's wonderful. Is it a drawing of you?"

"No! I don't have a dress like that, Mama!"

"Silly me! And you don't have quite so many pet butterflies, either."

"No, just a dog and cat." She sighed.

I imagined going home and tucking this girl and her butterflies into a manila folder, to which I'd later add a letter from the doctor, and perhaps one from the preschool teacher attesting to my respectability, accountability, morality. I winced at the juxtaposition. Surely the girl with the butterfly bouquet said everything that needed to be said. Why should joy have to build a case for itself?

I lay in bed that night and thought about how soft our landing had been so far. Compared to the gender refugees I had met from other states, I had lost virtually nothing when my child became a girl. A handful of acquaintances had said hurtful things, and I had let these people slip quietly out of my life. Most people just seemed to find us a curiosity, a learning opportunity, or a chance to demonstrate their liberal open-mindedness. Maybe they just didn't care one way or another what weird parenting experiment I was conducting. It wasn't *their* kid, after all.

I wondered how long this gentle ride could continue. Was the other shoe about to drop? Would my child still be viewed as a benign curiosity when she and her peers entered adolescence?

A FEW DAYS LATER a dad stopped me in the lobby at preschool to tell me something hilarious. His daughter had been insisting that *my* daughter had a *penis*! Weren't our kids just too much? Where did they come up with this stuff? *Ha ha, ha ha*, we laughed together.

I began rehearsing for the arrival of CPS. In my mind they came to the house over and over again, in excruciating detail. A dark daydream: There's a knock at the door. It's them. They have questions; they push past me and look around. I cringe at the mess in my living room. *Where is the child?* they ask. *Playing in her room,* I say. And then I pull out my phone to call my sister-in-law and beg her to come. *Now. Please. CPS is here.* She's an attorney, so hopefully she'll know what to do, what to say to *them.* I haven't done the safe folder. Why haven't I done the safe folder? I search for the butterfly girl drawing. I can't find it! My heart is pounding. Who called them? Why, oh why did I tell all the neighbors? Or was it a parent at school? Why isn't my sister-in-law answering? *We need you to get off the phone,* the CPS people say. I leave a message and hang up and attempt to explain. *She's always been this way,* I say.

*We need to see the child for ourselves,* they say. I can't allow this. What if they frighten her? What if *I* frighten her? *You can't take her,* I say. *You can't take her. I won't let you. I will never let you.* But they aren't listening. And they will not leave.

The scene stalls here, or resets, looping back to the moment they appear in my doorway, and plays out again with slight variations. But I can never seem to resolve it. It dangles and waits for next time, when I will once again fail to get them to listen or leave.

❖

FOR THE TIME BEING, things were quiet at preschool, but I didn't expect this to last. One school year had ended in the spring and in the fall two classes merged, which meant that half the kids knew that the girl named M. used to be called a boy, and the other half did not. The daughter of the dad who laughed at my child's penis apparently fell into this latter category.

One day my daughter came home and told me about Jack. "Jack says I'm a boy because I have a penis."

"How does Jack know that you have a penis?"

"Because he can see it when I go pee in the bathroom."

Of course. I had seen the arrangement: a bathroom with a single toilet and sink, attached to the classroom, right between the comfy reading couch and the dress-up corner. I think the bathroom had a door, but it was never closed. Kids lined up against the back wall of the bathroom while one used the toilet, another washed hands, and another dried them. It was a highly efficient system for coping with so many little bladders, so many germy hands. The alternative would likely have been a staff member devoted exclusively to potty patrol. But this assembly line of elimination offered zero privacy. Kids chatted to each other, to the child on the toilet, or just stared openly at the peeing child as they waited their turn. I appreciated the sweetness and innocence of it, but the terms of childhood had shifted for us, and the lack of privacy was now a problem.

"Well, obviously Jack is wrong," I said.

She rolled her eyes. "I know that!"

"Good, of course you do. Did you say that to Jack? Did you explain that girls can have penises?"

"I got the teacher. She told him."

"She told Jack that girls can have penises, too?"

"Yes."

"That's great. Good job getting the teacher to help you." I felt relief and gratitude for the teacher's support and for my child's utter confidence that she had it. But why hadn't the teacher told me about this incident with Jack? Hadn't I asked her to let me know if my child's gender change became an issue at school? And what would happen when Jack went home and explained all of this to his parents? "Do you want any more help with Jack?"

"Nope. It's all done now."

But it wasn't done. Jack's words had left their mark. We were driving home from preschool a few days later when she announced, "I want to be a normal girl."

"What do you mean?" I said, trying to sound curious and calm. "I think you *are* a normal girl."

"I mean long hair. And a bagina."

I reminded her that her hair would soon grow long, and that we had met many girls with penises at the support group. "Remember Gracie and Luna? Plus, Grandma and Aunt M. both have short hair, and they're both girls. Aren't *they* normal?"

"Yeah, but it's less normal. *Most* girls have a bagina and long hair. That's more normal."

She had me there. What could I say? "It's OK to be different?" Nice words, but being different wasn't always fun or easy. It made

Jack question your girlhood. And not just Jack, of course. Her own mother had mistaken her for a boy, and there was no doubt about which body part could be blamed for that.

I had already told her that the doctor could turn her penis into a vagina when she was older, if that's what she wanted. I'd also told her the doctor could give her medicines so she wouldn't grow a beard like her dad. We had started having these conversations months ago, because beards had continued to frighten her, "more than spiders and fire," she said. "Even more than monsters and bad guys." I reminded her about the things the doctors could do.

"But why do I have to wait until I'm grown up to get a bagina?" she whined.

I didn't know a lot about the specifics of the procedure, or precisely why she had to wait. So I said something about it being "not safe for kids." We both knew that my answer was insufficient.

"I WANT A BAGINA *NOWWWWW!!!!!*" she howled. The traffic roared around us as I pulled onto the freeway, and she sobbed and I discovered a whole new way that your heart can ache. My child was in pain, and I could not fix it for her, no matter how hard I tried or how badly I wanted to. Not yet, anyway, not for a long, long while.

I cursed little Jack, aware of how unfair this was. Jack was everyone. I was Jack. Yes, I had accomplished the switch to her new name and female pronouns. I had purchased her a lavishly girly new wardrobe. I was dutifully attending the support group meetings. And yet, my own behavior was still laced with subtle betrayals: While I often called her "angel" or "sweetheart," I also caught myself addressing my child as "dude" and "buddy," as if we were frat brothers. When a feminist friend chastised me for allowing Barbies in the house, I realized that it had not once occurred to me that I would need to school my daughter in the perils of sexism. And recently, I had come across a baby photo— one of my favorites, a close-up of my child's smiling little face— those big blue eyes staring straight into the camera, a Cheerio stuck to that dimpled chin. I swooned and pined for the chubby heft of this delicious child in my arms.

I showed M. "Look, this is you!"

She was delighted, too. "She is so cute!" she said of her younger self.

*She?*

We were looking at the same photo, but we were not seeing quite the same person. Without a doubt, I saw my baby boy. And I missed him, badly. But was I pining for my lost baby or my lost boy?

And if I did miss my "boy," what did that even mean? Why should love have a gender?

I CALLED CATHY from the support group. "Do you think it's significant that the only word my child consistently mispronounces is *vagina?*"

"I have no idea!" She laughed.

I told Cathy I felt like a traitor. How was I supposed to convince the world that I had a daughter when I was having doubts myself? And how could we be *sure—truly, absolutely sure*—that we actually had daughters? I confessed to her about missing my "son," and told her about the "boyish" behaviors I had noticed, the same things my family had pointed out: How active and physical my child was. Her obsession with LEGOs and sword fighting.

"Kind of a tomboy?" Cathy said.

"Sort of. But lots of girls like that stuff," I said. "I used to *love* sword fighting with my sister."

Cathy said her daughter was a tomboy, too. "She's into sci-fi and chess, and she hates clothes and everything traditionally girly. It's confusing, isn't it?"

"Endlessly."

"But I think the fact that our daughters are *not* so into traditionally 'girly' stuff actually makes a stronger case for them being transgender," Cathy said.

"How so?"

"Well, we know they don't want to be girls just so they can do girl stuff and wear girl clothes. They like a lot of boy stuff, so you'd think it would be easier for them to just be boys. But they aren't picking that easier route, because they simply can't. Their gender runs deeper than that."

"But that's the thing that gets me," I said. "What *is* gender? I just don't know if I believe in gender anymore, or at least not in the way I used to. If a girl can have any type of job, or wear any type of clothing, and even have a *penis*, what *is* a girl? I feel like the words *girl* and *boy* still mean something to other people that they don't mean for me anymore."

I told her how a group of women at my office were going out for "ladies' night" recently and I just kept thinking: *Why ladies' night'? Don't you see how meaningless these categories are?* "And don't you ever wonder if our kids might just be cool with being just, well, *kids*, if the world wasn't so hell-bent on stuffing them into categories?"

"That's why I'm so grateful for the blockers," she said. Cathy's daughter had been prescribed the medication by her doctor to block her puberty when she turned eleven, just before male puberty was about to kick into high gear. "It gives us some more time, for her to just be a kid, like you said, without having to decide anything and . . . in case she does change her mind."

"Do you think she will?"

Cathy paused. "I don't know. We're pioneers, right?"

I thanked her for the talk and was saying goodbye when she interrupted me. "One more thing, Marlo. I miss the 'boy,' too. I think we all do. We just can't tell *them* that."

No, we could not. How could I tell my child that I missed a person she would insist had never existed? And whose name and identity she had fought so hard to be free of? But in some odd and inexplicable way, I *did* miss my "son," and I caught confusing glimpses of him now and then: when I watched my child drift off to sleep or held my child in my arms and smelled . . . him.

Someday she will read this book, and perhaps, if she's a mother herself, she'll understand and forgive me for being grieved by her girlhood. But I don't think she'll be surprised. I think she noticed right away, or at least had her suspicions, because my daughter seemed to be taking extraordinary measures to cement her hard-won spot in the girl club. Pants were off the table; it had to be a skirt or a dress every day, without exception, even to ride her bike; even when we went sledding. If we really were pioneers, my child was certainly dressing the part, trudging up the mountain in skirts layered like petticoats, caked with snow. Along with pants, she also banned sports of all kinds, particularly ones played with balls. It didn't matter that most of the girls her age played on soccer teams. They also wore pants, of course, but she wasn't taking any chances.

It made me sad, but it made sense. Not long ago, her own mother—along with everyone else—had mistaken her for a boy. She wasn't about to let that happen again. Maybe Cathy was right and our kids really didn't have a choice. Why go to so much trouble to be a girl when you had to fight the whole world to be seen as one? Wouldn't just going with the "boy thing" be a whole lot easier, if you *could* swing it? Unless . . . you just couldn't.

AT THE NEXT SUPPORT GROUP, I had some more questions for the facilitator.

"You've been doing this for years, right?" I asked. "And you've known, what, hundreds of these kids?"

He nodded. "That's about right."

I asked him how many times he'd seen a kid like mine change her mind. "I mean, a kid who is absolutely adamant that they are a different gender," I said, "over an extended period of time, say . . . years, without wavering. Does that kid ever change back?"

"Once," he said. "I saw one child like yours switch back. But . . . they were getting too many broken bones."

"*Broken bones?*"

"At school, the other kids beat them up one too many times. It wasn't safe to be a girl anymore."

"But that doesn't count," I said. "That's not the same thing as really changing your mind."

He shrugged. "I guess not."

**M. (age six):** So, when I was little, my mama didn't know that I was a girl, and I didn't like that.

**Me:** Do you remember what you felt like when people called you a boy?

**M.:** I felt sad when people called me a boy name and didn't understand. I felt sad and didn't feel like who I was.

**Me:** How did it feel when people started to call you a girl?

**M.:** Well, now I feel happy that they understand.

# *Learn.*

I kept waiting for the other shoe to drop at preschool: a call from Jack's parents, another awkward tête-à-tête in the craft room with the teacher; but things were quiet. Maybe too quiet.

No one called, no one asked me why there was one less boy and one more girl in the Mountain Room. No one said a word. But of course, some of them had noticed. And of course, they were talking about us. In retrospect, it seems naive that I didn't realize this, and if we had skipped that end-of-year birthday party at the bouncy gym for a little girl whose name I can no longer recall, I might never have known how upsetting the situation was to the other moms.

As kids shrieked and scrambled up inflatable stairs and slid down inflatable slides, I tried to remember the name of the mom standing next to me. Nora? Nancy? "We found out about M. from our daughter," she said. For once, I was grateful for the noise and chaos of such a horrible place. Maybe she was, too. We both studied the entrance to a bouncy castle neither of our children were bouncing on.

"Oh?" I said.

"Yes," she said. Because of the open-door bathroom. "Madeleine kept saying, 'M. has a penis!' But I didn't believe her!" She laughed and glanced sideways at me, and I tried to laugh, too. "I mean, we were all talking about it when we went out for drinks—me, Cynthia, and Lisa—because all the kids were saying this. None of us believed them. We didn't know what to think until we talked to the teacher."

So they had asked the teacher if my child had a penis. And she said, yes, M. has a penis. M. used to be a boy.

"And you know, we all talked—me, Cynthia, and Lisa—and we *all* agreed that our only *problem* with it was that we hadn't been *told* and so we were calling our kids liars!"

I tried to nod sympathetically.

"When they were actually telling the truth! It felt really bad because we'd been accusing our kids of lying! If we had just *known*."

"That must have been very hard," I said.

"Yes!" She smiled and nodded vigorously, visibly relieved now that I had had things explained to me and I understood how hard this had been. "It was terrible!"

Now the air was clear, and fault had been laid squarely where it belonged: the mother and child who had actually been lying, and whose lie—that a girl could have a penis—had led to the injustice of false accusations against their own innocent children.

Had it been a mistake not to formally announce, and account for, the presence of a penis?

Was that my job? Was that my child's job? Would it always be? How many more times would my missteps and my child's genitals warrant discussion over drinks with Cynthias and Lisas? I imagined the three moms with appalling clarity, heads bent together over glasses of dark red wine, a candle flickering elegantly on the small table between them, eyes locked in their irresistible, affronted conspiracy. The image made me sick to my stomach, exactly like the time in seventh grade when Heidi Redding, the meanest and most popular girl in school, told me everyone thought I was stuffing my bra. And I had the exact same response: I smiled and pretended I was totally fine and then slunk away and hid behind the bouncy castle and sobbed my heart out.

Another thing Nora-Nancy had said was that it would have been really helpful if the school had done "a presentation or something." To explain about kids like mine. I knew I was

> **Me:** What does it mean to be transgender?
>
> **M. (age six):** Well, transgender is when, for example, if when you were born your mom and dad thought you were a boy because you had a penis, but in your heart you were a girl. So a girl with a penis would be a transgender person. Or, a boy with a bagina.

lucky that instead of wanting my kid kicked out of the school, the other parents actually wanted to learn about her. But it was also daunting. There was a whole world of parents out there—and teachers, doctors, coaches, and everyone else—who were going to want an explanation, and apparently it was going to be my job to provide it, at each new school, class, club, and playdate.

How was I supposed to explain something I barely understood myself? I had never felt uncomfortable with my identity as a girl, nor as a woman. This apparently fundamental component of my daughter's inner reality was something I could only imagine, like a food I had never tasted. So I tried to bridge the gap by reading.

I bought several memoirs written by transgender authors and began with one called *Conundrum* by Jan Morris. It was a slim paperback with the book's first sentence printed in large black letters right on the front cover: "I was three or perhaps four years old," wrote Morris, "when I realized that I had been born into the wrong body, and should really be a girl." The realization had first struck the author while she sat on the floor beneath the family's piano, listening to her mother play a song. "It is the earliest memory of my life," she wrote, and, "I have had no doubt about my gender since that moment."

Next I read *She's Not There* by Jennifer Finney Boylan, who described a childhood game played alone in the woods called "girl planet." "I was an astronaut who had crashed on an uninhabited world," wrote Boylan. "The thing was, though, that anybody who breathed the air on this planet turned into a girl." Boylan was also sitting on the floor, also with her mother, when *she* suddenly knew, at age three, that she was expected to be someone she was not. She recalls basking in a pool of sunlight beneath the ironing board while her mother ironed her father's shirts and upended her world with the prediction, "Someday you'll wear shirts like these." The small child knew immediately and instinctively that this was all wrong. "Since then," she wrote, "the awareness that I was in the wrong body, living the wrong life, was never out of my conscious mind—*never*."

I wondered where my child had been when she first knew that the world had mistaken her for a boy. Had I been with her? Had I been the one whose words had alerted her to this horrible error, when I called out to my beloved "boy"?

Unlike my child, Morris and Boylan kept their painful discoveries to themselves and carried them into adulthood. Over time, the "crushing burden," as Boylan called it, "only grew heavier, and heavier, and heavier." She described an "almost inexpressible degree of private grief," and "the nearly constant sense that I was the wrong person."

Morris felt like an "imposter," "a spy in a courteous enemy camp." It was, she wrote, "as though there were a piece missing from my pattern." Despite happy marriages and gratifying careers, Morris and Boylan found no relief until they both took the bold and risky steps to transition to living as women in their forties. "I would rather die young," Morris wrote, "than live a long life of falsehood."

I tracked down several more memoirs of gender transition and spent much of my free time devouring them. The authors came from wildly divergent backgrounds, separated by time, place, and circumstance. In spite of their differences, they all told, with heartbreaking eloquence, some version of the same story: a childhood of loneliness and longing, years of secret pain and shame, of fruitless attempts to somehow repress this overpowering inclination, and, ultimately, a blissful—if complex—relief, when at last, they finally took the steps that allowed them to walk the world as women.

I still didn't understand what it felt like to find yourself living a mislabeled life, wearing a body that felt like a betrayal, but these books had given me my best glimpse so far into the imagined inner world of my child. She was still only five years old. She could not yet describe for me the "crushing burden" she carried, or what it really felt like to have "a piece missing from her pattern." But these grown-up transgender women could—and they did. My gratitude for this gift is hard to overstate.

I felt something dissipate, as a long-clenched place inside me released.

"I'm sorry I didn't realize you were a girl, when you were littler," I said to my daughter as we snuggled up to read bedtime stories. "I'm sorry I didn't understand before."

She frowned, still focused on the picture book in her lap. She turned a page.

"I know it made you sad," I said.

She did not look up, but I detected a barely perceptible nod. Then I remembered something. I remembered that early on in my pregnancy, I was sure I was having a girl. I was so convinced

of this that I told my mom, who was equally convinced, and who
went out and bought a half-dozen baby girl outfits that later had
to be returned. I put my arm around my daughter and told her
this, hoping it would make her happy that my earliest thoughts
of her were girl ones.

"You knew I was a girl when I was in your tummy?" she said.

"I guess I did, yes."

A triumphant smile flashed across her face, then vanished.
"Why did you forget?"

Oh, my heart.

I explained how I'd been misled. Misled by things I had been
taught that turned out to be wrong: that all people with penises
were boys, and all those with vaginas were girls. "But I understand now," I said. "Mama gets it now."

Was this reassuring to her, or was it frightening, to be told that
your own mother had only very recently acquired such basic and
essential knowledge about humans like her? Perhaps it was both.

"I forgive you, Mama," she pronounced, returning to her book.

---

"I prayed for it every evening . . . while my betters I suppose were
asking for forgiveness or enlightenment, I inserted silently every
night, year after year throughout my boyhood, an appeal less graceful but no less heartfelt: 'And please, God, let me be a girl. Amen.'"
—Jan Morris, *Conundrum*

---

❖

"IT FEELS LIKE TIME is standing still," I wrote in my journal. "Why haven't things changed more?" Morris's book had first been published in 1974. By the time I picked it up, it was nearly forty years old. Morris was old enough to have served in the British Army in World War II. Her stories referenced telegrams, and her dreams of womanhood were modeled on Sonja Henie.

Jennifer Finney Boylan's book appeared a long generation later, with more recent references to the Vietnam War and the Grateful Dead, but with respect to their predicament, the world hadn't really changed much at all. Boylan was still trudging a nearly identical path to the one Morris had endured thirty years before, and finding it just as lonely, bewildering, and lacking in discernible signposts.

"Will my daughter one day find herself writing the same sad story?" I asked my journal. It wasn't as if these writers were the first to walk this path. My grandmother told me she remembered the excitement around Christine Jorgensen, whose transition in the early 1950s made for titillating headlines. *The New York Daily News* proclaimed: EX-GI BECOMES BLONDE BEAUTY. My parents recalled the hullabaloo in the 1970s over the transition of tennis star Renée Richards. But none of my friends had heard of Christine Jorgensen or Renée Richards; nor had they heard of Jennifer Finney Boylan, whose best-selling memoir had landed her an appearance on *Oprah* ten years before I read it.

Christine Jorgensen and Howard Knox

IT SEEMED THAT EACH GENERATION had to rediscover transgender people afresh, apparently unaware that their parents had once read the same salacious headlines. Or maybe the thinking was that the phenomenon was so rare as to occur only a handful of times per century. In any case it must represent a recent phenomenon, a modern fad. Surely this wasn't something our grandparents or great-grandparents would have encountered, but according to other books I had been reading, this was not so.

People living cross-gender lives had been found in the prehistoric grave sites of Europe, in the temple records of ancient Mesopotamia, in traditional cultures of Africa, in three-thousand-year-old Hindu texts, in the shocked accounts of

early European explorers who described fluid gender expression
in the native cultures from Alaska to Brazil, where a band of
women warriors attacked the invading Spaniards and inspired
the naming of the Amazon River. Someone like my daughter had
been an emperor of Ancient Rome. And an eighteenth-century
French spy in the Russian imperial court. And a soldier for the
Union Army in the American Civil War.

At this very moment, people like her were living openly in
Polynesia, where they are called *mahu* or *fa'afafine*. In Thailand,
they are the *katoey*, or "ladyboys." In India, they are called *hijra*
and carry out spiritual functions, including the blessing of
newborns.

I began to realize that there was no time or place in which people like my child had *not* existed. The more this truth sunk in,
the more confusing and
shocking I found the veil
of near-absolute silence
regarding their existence.
Jennifer Finney Boylan
had expressed it perfectly
in her memoir. "Even
now," she wrote in 2003,
"a discussion of transgendered people frequently
resembles nothing so
much as a conversation
about *aliens*. . . . Has the

Chevalier d'Éon, a French diplomat and
spy who successfully infiltrated the court
of Empress Elizabeth of Russia

government known about them for years and kept the whole business secret? Where do they come from, and what do they want? Have they been living secretly among us for years?"

---

**American Psychological Association**

**FACT SHEET: Gender Diversity and
Transgender Identity in Children[5]**

Although there is more recent awareness of gender diverse and transgender children in our society today, these children are not part of a "new" phenomenon. Cross-gender behavior has existed throughout history in every continent and within a wide range of cultures for thousands of years. Although no consensus exists on the etiology of gender diversity, neurobiological evidence for sex-specific brain differences in transgender people is being explored. One's gender identity is very resistant, if not immutable, to any type of environmental intervention.

---

Of course, they had. Hiding—or just living—in plain sight, like the support group facilitator I had not guessed was transgender. Perhaps one of them was my barista or my coworker or a neighbor. This remarkable thought had never occurred to me, just as it had never occurred to me that one of them might be my child. Boylan was right. It did feel like a cover-up. And it had to end.

I wanted to shout it through a megaphone from a rooftop. I wanted to call the editors of newspapers and alert my senators. I wanted it inserted in the parenting books, alongside vaccinations and nut allergies, because if we were at risk of losing 40 percent of transgender kids to this urgent, invisible force, then it was far deadlier to our young than measles or tree nuts. And yet almost no one was speaking of it.

I had tried and failed to find a single online article or blog written by a parent with a young transgender child. This seemed implausible—wasn't *everything* on the internet? But "everything" didn't seem to include us yet. All I could find were a handful of blogs about feminine boys like the one in the *My Princess Boy* picture book my child had hurled across the room. As far as I could tell, the entire internet told no tales written by parents like me. It was time to change that.

I turned to a new page in my journal and wrote a short essay with the highlights of our story and titled it "My Penis Girl." I found a free blogging website and signed up with the pseudonym "gendermom" and posted my little essay. I didn't share it or tell anyone about it, so maybe nobody else would ever read it. But at least the internet would include us now.

A few days later, I saw that my post had been featured on the blogging website's home page. It had over one hundred comments.

*Your child sounds just like mine. I'm so lost and scared. Thank you so much for writing about this.*

*Sad Sad Sad . . . you will be judged by the Almighty God for what you are endorsing. God gave you a boy and he will be a boy until he dies.*

*All throughout my childhood I was beaten and humiliated for try-ing to dress or act female because I was born with a male body. To have parents like you and to be a trans kid today is the stuff my dreams were made of! I am so jealous of your daughter.*

*Quite disgusting. gendermom is a nutcase at best.*

*Never give up . . . even when it gets harder . . . and it will.*

# *Find your tribe.*

Nearly a year had passed since the switch, and family, friends, and neighbors were slowly succumbing to the new name and pronouns. There were no dramatic shifts to signal their acceptance, no sudden avalanches of understanding that I could perceive, and definitely no confident proclamations on the validity of her girlhood, as there once had been on her supposed boyhood. But over time, I was pleased to see, she was slowly wearing them all down, like the drip-drip-drip of water against a rock. Even my nephews, who had initially objected to their mother's name being appropriated by their cousin, gave way, and the youngest one announced that M. was "still pretty fun, even as a girl."

One of our neighbors began dropping by regularly with fairy-themed gifts. No one dropped by from CPS, though I still silently rehearsed for their arrival. If they did show up, the five-year-old child they would find would certainly look the part. She was still enforcing her no-pants policy, and although her hair wasn't as long as it was in her Rapunzel self-portraits, it now grazed the top of her shoulders and was, without a doubt, "girl hair." She was evidently pleased with it, pausing to fluff it and primp whenever she encountered a mirror.

She hadn't asked for a "bagina" in several months and seemed to have reached a lighthearted truce with her anatomy. "It's pretty silly and wiggly," she said of her penis. "But I *don't* like how it stands up straight sometimes."

"That must be annoying," I said, full of genuine sympathy.

"Very," she said.

While she wrapped up her final weeks of preschool, I spent my time fretting about kindergarten. It should have been simple. We lived just a few blocks from a public school with a great reputation. They said families moved into the neighborhood just to be in its attendance zone. There was even a "walking school bus" that paraded past our house each morning, with parents taking turns shepherding a flock of the neighborhood's children along the sidewalk to the school.

The problem was, I had heard too many stories of some combination of principals and parents and peers making the life of a small trans child at school a misery. All it would take, I reasoned, were a couple of families to make our lives hell: demanding that she use the boys' bathroom; forbidding their children from speaking to her; spreading stories about us to the other parents, the community, perhaps even to local media. And, as I'd learned in preschool, even parents who might accommodate us would still be discussing us and would demand explanations. My daymares of CPS dropping by were joined by elementary school disaster scenarios featuring a mob of outraged parents wielding smartphones and social media in place of pitchforks.

I heard from other parents at the support group that some of their kids were homeschooled, but I was a single mom with a full-time job, so that option was off the table. I started looking into private schools, thinking that perhaps a small school with an overtly supportive stance on diversity might be a safer spot for us, but I didn't know how I'd manage to come up with the tuition.

We were at a family potluck for the support group when M. solved the school problem for us. She had wandered off in the crowd, and I found her at a table across the room, climbing onto an empty chair and shouting at the girl across from her. "How old are *you*?"

"I'm twelve," the girl said shyly. She picked up a potato chip from her paper plate and nibbled its edge.

A woman next to her with rosy cheeks and lime-green glasses smiled up at me, "Is this your kitty cat?"

For some reason M. was dressed as a cat, in a black leotard and tights, and a headband with kitty ears. There were black whiskers drawn across her pale cheeks.

"Yes, she is mine. Sorry, did she take someone's seat?"

"No way! She's *perfect.*"

"*Purrrr-fect*, you mean," the kitty said, eyeing the older girl's paper plate. "Can I have some of your potato chips?"

The rosy-cheeked woman slapped the seat next to her. "Sit down, Mama. We definitely need to get to know you two better. I'm Alice." Alice sent the girls off to scour treats from the buffet table and told me her story. She had been coming to the group since her daughter Olivia was six years old. "She was putting things on her head to make long hair," Alice said. "Towels, pants, anything. Finally, we came to the group and put the pieces together." When she transitioned from Oliver to Olivia, Alice's daughter was just finishing up kindergarten at a private school I had heard of but hadn't considered because of the location. It was a half-hour drive in the opposite direction from my commute to work, but Alice made a powerful case.

"The school was wonderful about it," she said. "They're super committed to diversity. And as a white mama to two adopted Black kids, it's been awesome for us." Plus, she said all her lesbian friends sent their kids there. Olivia had moved on to middle school, but her two younger brothers still attended the school. As it turned out, we were nearly neighbors. She drove by our house on her way to the school every morning. We could carpool.

It was tempting, but it made very little practical sense. Even with Alice's help, I'd be adding hours of commuting to my week. Not to mention that the private-school tuition would likely eat up most of my savings and discretionary income, even if I split the cost with my ex and the school offered us financial aid.

Our daughters returned to the table, holding paper plates piled high with potato chips and cookies. M. set hers down, then climbed into Alice's lap and meowed. "Would you like a cookie?" she asked.

"I can drive your little kitty cat to school every morning," Alice said, helping herself to a cookie.

I grabbed one, too. "Sounds like we have a plan."

❖

ALICE MUST HAVE BEEN a good omen, because in the summer that followed, the summer prior to kindergarten, it felt like the world was beginning to open its arms to embrace our children—or at least acknowledge their existence.

In June, a little girl just like mine was all over the news. A Colorado school district had barred transgender six-year-old Coy Mathis from using the girls' bathroom. Her family fought back, sued the district, and won. Little Coy had appeared with her parents on Katie Couric's talk show, and around the same time, Barbara Walters profiled another transgender girl, eleven-year-old Jazz Jennings, on *20/20*. In August, the state of California passed a law mandating that transgender K–12 students be allowed access to the bathrooms, locker rooms, and sports teams that aligned with their gender identities.

I wrote an excited post on my new blog. "Did we really win the social justice lottery? Is society *really* getting around to addressing transgender civil rights just in the nick of time to save my child from the hell endured by previous generations of trans folks?" It seemed too good to be true.

My conversations began to shift. I didn't have to spend so much time convincing everyone that unicorns were real, because now they had seen one themselves, sitting on the couch across from Katie Couric or Anderson Cooper. And they all wanted me to know about it. I would get five different emails from friends and relatives with links to the same article or video about Coy or Jazz or another kid like mine. I always wrote back and thanked them and pretended theirs was the only one, because I was so glad and grateful.

Around the same time, I received another email reflecting this magical new world. It was from Peter, a software developer who had recently been hired by my company. It said, "Since we last talked, I am about half a year into a gender transition and am now living full-time as a woman. Please refer to me as Kate from now on."

I had never actually met "Peter" in person, but I badly wanted to meet Kate. As far as I knew, I had never met a transgender woman. Of course, I must have unknowingly run across lots of trans people over the course of my life, but I had not once sat down to talk with a woman I knew to be transgender. And if I was going to raise a transgender child, it would probably be a good idea for me to meet some people like her, rather than just reading about them in books. Maybe people like Kate could even help me understand my child better and give me a glimpse of what her future might look like.

I wrote back to Kate. I congratulated her on her transition and told her about my five-year-old transgender daughter and suggested we meet. Then I worried. Had I overstepped? Maybe Kate would be offended at being asked to be my token trans friend. She replied and said she'd love to meet, and we set a date for dinner.

"My brain *loves* estrogen," Kate told me, as we bent over steaming plates of pad thai. She couldn't believe how happy she was, she said, how *right* things felt now after so many years of everything feeling all wrong. She was nearly thirty, but reminded me of a teenager, and in a way, she *was* one: I had heard that transition could feel like a second puberty, with all those new hormones coursing through your body. "I'm pretty obsessed with clothes," she said. "And I'm boy crazy!"

When she transitioned, she had become the only woman on her team of software developers at work. "They don't let me finish my sentences anymore. I get interrupted constantly."

"Welcome to womanhood," I said. We groaned and laughed and toasted with our water glasses. I complimented her pretty outfit. She told me she was dating a lot, and that in fact she had a date later that evening with a guy she'd met online.

I worried out loud. "Are you being careful?"

She promised she was. She patted her purse and told me she always carried mace with her. When we said goodbye I hugged her tightly and reminded her again about being careful. I didn't want to release this boy-crazy teenager alone into the city at night.

"I'll be all right," she promised.

A couple of weeks later I took my daughter to meet Kate for pizza. Kate seemed nervous around her, like she wasn't sure how to talk to a young child. But my daughter dug Kate. She kept getting up from her chair and walking around the table to hug her. Kate blushed each time.

Kate had given me permission to tell M. that she was transgender, and I had told my daughter that Kate "was living as a boy until last year, when she realized that she was actually a girl." Was *that* why M. was giving her so many hugs? Was she worried about her, too? Or was she claiming her as one of her own?

On the drive home, M. said we should definitely have Kate over to our house to play very soon.

KATE TOLD ME ABOUT a newly formed group of local transgender activists. They met every Tuesday in a basement office in a much hipper part of town than the one I lived in. Tuesdays happened to be one of the evenings my daughter always spent with her dad. It seemed meant to be.

I drove to the meeting alone after work. They were just getting started when I arrived. I grabbed the last free seat at the table as the person sitting next to me said, "Let's go around the room and do names and pronouns," inviting me to go first.

"I'm Marlo, and I'm, um, a *she*," I said, hoping I'd done it correctly. I realized I had already assumed I could guess the pronouns of everyone in the room. I was soon proved wrong. There were about a dozen of us, mostly *she*s, a couple of *he*s, plus a *they*, and someone who used a pronoun I'd never heard before. Clearly, I had a lot to learn.

I had called ahead to ask if it was OK for a family member of a transgender person to participate in the group, even if I wasn't trans myself. "Absolutely," I was told. "We love having allies join us."

After we finished introductions, I was asked if I wanted to tell the group a little bit about myself, since I was new. "Well, I have a transgender daughter," I said. "She's five years old. And I'm here to support her." Half the room had been looking down at their phones. When I spoke, heads popped up. Every face was now turned in my direction.

Someone began to clap softly, and the rest joined in. "I wish *my* mom were here," said a very young person sitting across from me in baggy denim overalls who had given a sweetly fanciful-sounding name, something like Skylark, and she/her pronouns.

"I do *not* wish *my* mom were here," said another beautiful young *she*, rolling her eyes.

I thought about all the grim statistics I had been hearing about transgender people. People like my daughter endured sky-high rates of just about every form of statistically measurable suffering: homelessness, unemployment, violence and abuse, mental illness and drug addiction. These were the results of living in a society that barely recognized your existence, let alone your humanity. I looked around the table as they clapped for me and wondered if I'd be able to bear hearing the stories these young people might have to tell me. And then I was hit with the painful thought that until very recently, I might have been one of their persecutors. Until very recently, if I had encountered someone like Skylark, with her low-pitched voice and stubbly chin, I would have thought she was weird.

I was glad when they stopped clapping. I didn't say much for the rest of the meeting, but I did sign up to help out with the transgender pride march they were planning for that June.

Skylark walked up to me afterward. "You are fucking amazing," she said. "My mom kicked me out of the house. Can I have a hug?"

ON A CLOUDY SEATTLE EVENING in June, we shuffled through the blocked-off city streets with several hundred other marchers behind a big banner that said TRANS PRIDE. We chanted and cheered and waved signs, then gathered in a park for speeches. Local transgender people had been participating in the city's huge Pride parade for years, but this year the community represented by the T finally had its own event. I had helped write the press releases and was happy to see a couple of local TV news crews there. It felt important, even historic, like the start of something. I didn't bring my daughter. She could join this fight when she was older.

When it got dark, a band played and people danced in front of the stage. I spotted Skylark among them, laughing and shaking her hips, barefoot in the grass.

"Someday I'll tell my daughter about this," I wrote on my blog, "and she'll know how much I love her."

---

In 2011, the National Transgender Discrimination Survey published the sobering results of their survey of more than six thousand transgender and gender-nonconforming people. The report, titled "Injustice at Every Turn," found a pervasive pattern of discrimination against trans people in every arena of their lives: In childhood homes and schools, in "harsh and exclusionary workplaces, at the grocery store, the hotel front desk, in doctors' offices and emergency rooms, before judges and at the hands of landlords, police officers . . . [and] health care workers."

Seventy-eight percent of those surveyed reported having been harassed in school, and 98 percent were harassed at work. Twenty-five percent lost their jobs because of their gender identity. They were four times as likely as the general population to be living in extreme poverty and twice as likely to have been homeless. Fifty-seven percent had experienced significant family rejection. A heart-breaking 41 percent of those surveyed reported attempting suicide, with "African American transgender respondents faring far worse than all others in most areas examined."

—*Injustice at Every Turn: A Report of the National Transgender Discrimination Survey*, a survey of 6,450 transgender and gender-nonconforming people, published in 2011[6]

---

❖

I STARTED TO RECEIVE EMAILS from people who had read my blog. Their raw honesty often took my breath away. I did my best to write back to all of them.

> gendermom, I wasn't fortunate enough to know at a young age like your daughter did. Yes, I knew I didn't quite fit, I knew I wasn't quite right. But it wasn't until after puberty hit that I started having these wishes to rip the breasts off of my chest, or slice my large thighs off. The older I got, the worse the feelings got. It wasn't until I was 17 that I realized what

"transgender" meant, and I embraced the fact that even though I'm very feminine, I can still be a boy. If possible, could you tell your daughter I said hello and give her a big hug for me? I am so proud of her and her strength.

Dear gendermom, I, too, am transgendered, 57 years old and nine years postoperative. I fell in that generational gap of time where I was able to make my choice late in life, but lose the entirety of my life: My career as a high school teacher, a life with my children and my grandchildren (my daughters have never let me meet my eight grandchildren). I miss them so! I live underground now. Even my boyfriend of seven years does not know about my past. Reading about your daughter made me cry, and deeply so. How I wish I began this life at a later time and place. Oh, how I wish I could begin again.

gendermom, I first realized I was a woman on the inside at age seven. Like most transsexual people born when I was, I transitioned late in life—at the age of 48. If only I could have stopped all the raging testosterone that turned me into Sasquatch. I am 6'5" and hairy as a caveman with a very deep voice. There's no fixing me.

Dear gendermom, I think your blog is terrific. I am writing to ask if you would consider doing a sensitive interview about your child. I write for the British tabloid newspapers and take pride in covering thought-provoking issues in a nonsensational way for a wide audience. Transgender issues are still very much a taboo and misunderstood. I feel your story would potentially make a real difference. Is this something you might consider doing? We would need photos of your child both before and after. There would be a fee for you.

gendermom, will you be at the conference this summer? If so, I'd sure love to meet you!

I *was* planning to attend the conference. I had been hearing about this conference since I first started attending the support group. Gender Odyssey was one of the largest gatherings in the country for transgender people, and it happened to be held in my hometown each summer, thanks to the efforts of the same unassuming support group facilitator who had been guiding me wryly and gently for months. On the first day, he stood at a podium at the downtown convention center and welcomed a cheering crowd to the thirteenth annual event.

For the next three days, I sat with parents like me on folding chairs in windowless conference rooms, sharing stories and survival tips and tissue boxes. A young dad told us how the kids at school were bullying his nine-year-old trans daughter. "They call her a 'He-She,'" he said, his voice breaking. "How can they do that to my little girl? Why won't the teachers stop them?"

"Our doctor refused to let my teen daughter get a blocker," a mother told us, "and her voice dropped. So now she refuses to speak in public. I have to order for her in restaurants."

"Who will love my child?" another mother lamented. "What if he gets rejected when his girlfriend finds out he's not a 'real man'? Who will love him?" Around the room, shoulders slumped.

Families had driven hundreds of miles and taken long flights to be there, many of them for their very first encounters with parents of another child like their own. In the hallways between sessions, tearful mothers embraced; tearful fathers gave each other warm, manly thumps on the back. In the conference center's massive ballroom, an elaborate day camp hosted scores of young children engaged in messy art projects and rowdy games. Groups of teens roamed the halls in packs, immersed in a conference all their own. If the support group had been a village, this felt like a small nation.

I hadn't brought my daughter on day one, thinking it would all be too much, but now, she was missing. I wanted to introduce her to the families I was meeting and hold her in my arms during breaks. The next morning on the drive downtown, I tried to explain to her that there would be lots of kids like her at the day camp, but she only seemed interested in the activities on offer: "Did you say they have a big princess area? With thousands of gowns?" I may have exaggerated a bit to get her out of bed early on a Saturday.

"Yes, there is a huge princess area," I said. "The biggest one I've ever seen." She squealed and kicked her legs against her booster seat. Maybe she didn't need to know just yet why an entire conference had been built around people like her. Maybe all *she* needed at five years old was to play, carefree, with the other village children, while her mother built alliances and prepared for battle.

Because battles lay ahead, for all of us. The experts presenting at the conference were making that very clear. A therapist told us that bullying was a virtual given. "It's going to happen," she said, "so you have to prepare your kids for how they'll respond."

A lawyer outlined the flimsy and confusing patchwork of laws and regulations, varying wildly across states, counties, and school districts, which in most cases failed to provide our children with even the most basic legal protections.

A social worker warned that our children's schools would invariably attempt to sidestep the "bathroom issue" by suggesting that our kids use the nurse's bathroom. "Don't fall for this 'solution,'" she said. "It singles out your child and it never works." They end up holding it all day, she said, to avoid drawing attention to themselves. "I can't tell you how many of these kids get urinary tract infections from refusing to pee at school." A roomful of mothers tutted at this unhealthy state of affairs.

---

"There has actually never been one case—not one case published—where a kid has socially transitioned and then decided that they were going to roll with their birth gender, and was harmed by it.

No one's ever even clinically talked about that, because it just doesn't happen.

Some kids have said, 'Yeah, it was kind of awkward to tell my parents that I'd changed my mind,' but they never say, 'My life was ruined and I couldn't go to college.'"

—Dr. Johanna Olson-Kennedy, Medical Director,
Center for Transyouth Health and Development at Children's
Hospital Los Angeles, August 2015, Gender Odyssey Conference,
Seattle, Washington

---

IN A SESSION on medical interventions, a doctor told us that at least we had science on our side. "Research going back to the 1970s shows that gender constancy is intact by three to five years old," she said. But she added that her clinic was also full of kids who didn't freak out about their gender—or get their parents' attention—until the full weight of the wrong puberty hit them later on. "Thirteen-year-old trans boys who get their periods are *not* happy campers, let me tell you." Kids came to her clinic wanting to die rather than go through the wrong puberty, she said. Those who claimed that these were just spoiled teens trying to piss off their parents, or that it was a passing phase that could be ignored, needed to wake up and smell the science. Kids were dying. And this meant that blockers constituted a life-saving medical intervention.

Then she explained how blockers worked. When puberty was about to kick in, our kids had two options. They could have regular injections, or have a tiny implant inserted under the skin, generally on the upper arm. Both contained a medication that essentially pressed the pause button on puberty.

She said it was safe: It had been used for decades to slow things down for kids exhibiting "precocious puberty"—seven-year-old boys growing mustaches, for example, or six-year-old girls growing breasts.

She said it was reversible: Stop the shots or remove the implant, and puberty cranks right back into gear as if nothing had happened.

And, she said, it was expensive: The doctor held up a small plastic box containing an implant. "If you are an adult man with prostate cancer, this is basically free. Because your insurance will cover it. But if you're a trans kid, this little guy will set you back ten thousand dollars or more. I'll pass it around so you can see it for yourself."

As this pricey little miracle made its way around the room, she explained why blockers were such a godsend: By pausing puberty without requiring hormones or other medical interventions that might have lasting effects, they bought time, giving teens—and their jittery parents—a chance to consider whether they were all really on board with this transgender thing.

When it made its way to me, I took the implant out of the box and held it in my palm. It was a tiny white cylinder, about the size of half a toothpick. I tried to imagine it embedded in my daughter's skinny arm. Despite the hefty price tag, it seemed preferable to regular injections; my daughter was terrified of needles. I wondered if I should take the money from the British tabloid to pay for all this.

"I wasn't doing this five years ago," the doctor told us. She explained that until recently, puberty blocking was only available to a handful of transgender children in the Netherlands. Our kids would be part of a historic cohort, the first generation of American children to be given the option of avoiding a puberty that felt like a betrayal. She paused for a deep breath and looked out at her audience of terrified, history-making parents. "We are living in the future."

Meanwhile, the present—and the past—were gathered nearby, sitting in folding chairs in identical rooms in an adjacent wing of the convention center, participating in the adult version of the conference. The adult meetings were separate from the ones for parents, but we passed one another in the halls between sessions, exchanging shy smiles on the escalators and standing in line for lunch. I ran into some of my pals from the Trans Pride march, but the adults who caught my eye at the conference were older: women my mother's age, who might themselves be grandparents, too. I thought of the email from the woman who had described herself as a Sasquatch and wondered if she was there. I saw no one who looked anything like a caveman. I just kept seeing my daughter, grown-up. And I imagined them small, like she was now. They noticed us, too. I caught them watching my child, studying her.

I had so many questions for them. What was it like when they were her age? How did they ever find the courage to transition later in life, in a world like this? Did they see themselves in my daughter? I wanted to tell them that I thought I saw the little girls they once were. That I thought they were beautiful, because I did. But I had no idea how to begin such a conversation.

I ran into Cathy at the lunch break and tried to explain my frustration. Shouldn't our children be meeting their elders?

"It's complicated," she said. Cathy said her own daughter had been upset when she first saw some of the adult trans women at the conference a few years ago. She had said to her mom, "I'm not going to look like that, am I?"

"Oh no," I said, utterly deflated—for myself, for Cathy, for our daughters, for their elders who came of age long before this era of blockers, conferences, and other miracles.

Cathy went on: "Plus a lot of the new parents here, they get nervous seeing the older trans people," she said. "They find them kind of . . . strange and intimidating."

"But they are just like our kids," I said. "Or they once were."

"I know."

LATER THAT DAY, at the "teen panel," a dozen transgender teenagers told their stories to a room packed with parents hanging on their every word. Like me, these parents of young children had heard the grim statistics about transgender adolescents: rates of depression, self-harm, drug abuse, and suicide many times higher than any other group their age. We were there looking for hope.

A nonbinary teen broke down crying. "I just wish my dad would *see* me." A roomful of parents leaned forward helplessly in our seats. A leggy trans teen girl with Barbie-blond hair told us she wanted a family someday. "I can't wait to be a mom," she said. She had just started estrogen and was excited about growing breasts. Her parents had been very supportive. But not a soul at her school knew she was transgender.

"Not even your best friends?" someone in the audience called out.

"Are you kidding?" She laughed. "It's junior high! If I tell even one of them, the whole school will know by the next day."

She shrugged and passed the mic to the girl next to her, who beamed and told us, "I'm in love. And my boyfriend totally accepts me, just as I am." She swooned, and the roomful of parents swooned with her.

BY THE FINAL DAY of the conference, my mind was full. I hatched a plan with a mom I'd just met to skip out of the last session and get a drink. We went to a bar across the street from the convention center and sipped our beers and talked only of our kids. It turned out they were almost exactly the same age, both five and a half. But they were mirrors of each other, traveling in opposite directions along the gender binary—mine boy to girl, hers girl to boy. I found her predicament fascinating, intimidating. I tried to imagine raising a boy with a vagina. How would that work? It sounded incredibly difficult.

"I can't imagine raising a transgender girl," she said. "That sounds so much harder."

"I was just thinking the same thing about you!"

We laughed at ourselves and then debated who had it easier. I admitted I was even more intimidated by the nonbinary kids. My brain was just beginning to wrap itself around the idea that you could toggle between the two genders I had grown up with. But a *third* gender? How would I explain *that* to the grandparents?

"I don't know," she said. "I guess everything's hard when you haven't done it yet."

At the end of the weekend my daughter announced that the conference had been her "favorite time ever." She said we should go back again next week so she could make another fairy wand.

I told her I had loved the conference, too, and that we would definitely go to the next one. I said that I had loved meeting other parents with kids like her. "Did you enjoy meeting other girls who were transgender?"

"Huh?"

"Girls like you, with penises. Did you meet some?"

She narrowed her eyes at my silly question. "How would I know *that*, Mama?"

❖

I RECEIVED MORE EMAILS for gendermom.

> Your blog is so honest and open that I wanted to reach out.
> Our talk show is in national syndication and is produced
> by the same team behind "Maury" and "The Jerry Springer
> Show." I am a producer working on an hour devoted to Trans
> youth. We are taping our program next Friday and hope you
> and your daughter will consider participating. We cover all
> guest travel & accommodations to New York City. I hope to
> talk with you very soon.

First the British tabloids; now a national television show. Were we really this interesting? I found some clips of the talk show on YouTube. I didn't bother watching them after I read the titles:

*I cheated on my husband with my daughter's girlfriend!*

*Cosmetic surgery disasters!*

*The Man with Five Wives!*

Were we really this *strange*?

THEN I READ the next email.

> Dear gendermom,
>
> Please forgive me for writing to you directly, but I thought I would share a little bit of my story. I certainly never had the advantage that your very lucky daughter will have, but I can tell you that life is fulfilling for grown-up transgender girls. I have had a 38-year career in public affairs, own my own home, have been with the same man for 35 years, and this year I will turn 63 years old. I began my transition at the ripe age of 24 in 1975. It was that or live my life in absolute misery.
>
> The world seems to have a problem with us, but I do not care what our society says and simply rejoice in living my life as the woman I am! Your daughter has a very promising future ahead of her.
>
> Bless you.
> Lauren

I WROTE BACK to the New York TV producer and said, "No thank you." I said no to the British tabloid money, too. I'd have to figure out another way to pay for the blockers. Then I replied to Lauren, who was transgender and not strange at all. In fact, she sounded nothing like the stereotypes I realized were still housed in my head, thanks in large part to the very type of tabloids and TV show I had just turned down. Lauren was no more strange than we were, and she was living what sounded like a wonderful life. I needed to hear more about that. I needed to hear about her happy transgender life, and about the one she envisioned for my daughter.

Dear Lauren,

You made my day. My daughter is about to start kindergarten and the truth is, I'm scared to death.

# Secure the perimeter.

Alice's diversity-friendly private school had offered us a generous chunk of financial aid, and my ex agreed to split the rest. My daughter had a snazzy new set of clothes and a Tinker Bell backpack with a matching lunch box. Alice had been true to her word; she was on deck to drive my five-and-a-half-year-old kitty cat to school every morning.

I drove her myself on the first day. I hovered with the other parents while our kids stuffed their backpacks into cubbies, and then we sat with our children in our laps reading to them until the teacher gently shooed us out the door. We lingered in the hall, misty-eyed and nervous, and introduced ourselves.

"I'm Marlo, and my daughter is M.," I heard myself say. Using the word *daughter* felt both natural and strange. She *was* my daughter, I was now convinced. Saying so was true, but it was incomplete, which was the part that felt strange. Because we had decided not to tell.

Months of planning had gone into this decision. It started in the spring with tentative emails to the school principal. "I wanted to make sure you were aware that my daughter is transgender," I had written. "And Will and I are so grateful that our child will be joining this welcoming and diverse community. Could you meet with us before the school year begins in order to discuss some practical details?"

I knew from Alice that the school was primed to welcome us. They prided themselves on their reputation for diversity in all forms. They had embraced little Olivia's transition from male to female without incident. No one had bullied or excluded her. No one had objected to her using the girls' bathroom. I also knew from Alice that her child was the first and only transgender child the school had so far encountered. Her transition had occurred five years earlier, with a different principal in charge and a teacher who no longer taught there. Also, when she transitioned, everyone already knew her. They knew and loved her as Oliver in kindergarten before meeting her as Olivia in first grade. This must have helped to win them over. This also meant that there had been no possibility of keeping anything under wraps.

By contrast, we had a blank slate. Nobody at the school knew us except for Alice, who knew better than to breathe a word. Her own daughter had moved on to an all-girls middle school where she opted to be completely "stealth." None of the other girls there had any idea that their classmate was transgender. But Olivia was twelve, not five.

Olivia was old enough to know what much of the world thought of people like her. She also understood how quickly secrets could spread and that once it was out, there was no putting it back; that kids did not generally get nicer as they got older, but often the reverse.

If we told everyone now, would we regret it later? Would my daughter hate me in fifth grade when all her classmates knew she had a penis? If we didn't tell, would the other parents get angry when they found out, like they did in preschool? Would her friends feel betrayed? Would harboring such a secret even be healthy, or possible, for such a young child? If I advised her to hide, would I be sending the message that she ought to be afraid? Or, possibly worse, ashamed? If I advised her to share, could I keep her safe?

"I almost wish everyone just already knew," I complained to Cathy. "Then the choice would be out of our hands."

"I don't envy you that decision," she said. Like Olivia, her daughter had remained at the same school after her transition. "You know who your friends are pretty quick."

I told her I'd asked to meet with the principal and was working on my pitch. "Alice says he should be sympathetic but may not know much about trans issues."

"Yeah, well, most people don't."

THE PRINCIPAL LOOKED TIRED, like he'd sat through far too many meetings like this with worried parents like us. Alice told me he was expected to retire soon. Will and I took turns providing a brief backstory, explaining how she had "always just been this way," how she had told us at age three that she was actually a girl. We had gotten used to doing this—providing evidence that she really was trans, making the case that she really was a girl. Especially when we needed someone's help, which we did now. Badly.

The principal took in our story, nodding and faintly smiling. So far, so good.

Will switched to logistics. "We'd like to talk about whom we tell," Will said. "Obviously, her teacher will know." He smiled winningly at the young woman who sat next to the principal. She smiled shyly back. She had hardly spoken since we sat down and introduced ourselves, which was making me nervous. Was she up for this?

"Great, great." The principal tap-tap-tapped his pencil on the table. "Excellent idea to plan ahead on this. So, we'll tell the whole staff?"

My ex and I shook our heads in unison. We had conferred briefly and decided to start out with telling only on a need-to-know basis. We could always share more widely later. Why not start out by erring on the side of caution? "We feel pretty strongly that this is our child's private information," Will said.

The principal scratched his chin. "The school nurse? In case . . . something happens."

We had expected this suggestion. It sort of made sense. But what was going to happen? A medical emergency that involved her private parts? That seemed unlikely. It wasn't asthma or a bee allergy; it was a penis. But I got it. Because it was a body part, and that made it sort of a medical thing, right?

We agreed to telling the school nurse. I looked across the table at the teacher. She was taking notes. She looked nervous. And young. Definitely younger than me. I wanted her to say something reassuring, something about how it was going to be fine, how she was going to protect my daughter.

"We want her to have people who know that she's transgender, who can make her feel safe," I said, looking at her. "And who she can go to if she needs something."

"Yes, allies," Will said.

The principal nodded. The teacher wrote something down.

"It would probably be good to have some plans in place," I said. "Like, what happens if another parent complains? Or asks about our child's gender? Or if the kids start gossiping about her?"

"Those are really good questions," the principal said. "Would you like us to come to you about these things, if they happen?"

"Yes . . . but I don't really have the answers. I'm not an educator or a gender expert. I'm just a mom."

I brought up the idea of a gender training session. I'd heard from the parents at the support group about what a difference this could make in winning over skeptical teachers and establishing guidelines for how to respond to parents who complained or asked nosy questions about private parts. I had brought along the business card of a social worker who offered such training to local schools.

"It might help the staff and the other parents understand about kids like ours at the school." I said *kids*—plural—on purpose. I didn't want them to think I was requesting all this for my one special snowflake. Surely ours wasn't the only child at the school who was dancing to the beat of her own gender. Plus, the training wasn't just about transgender kids, I explained. It was about looking at how we *all* express our gender in unique ways—tomboys and "princess boys" and everything in between.

The principal gave me the kind of earnest, silent nod you give someone when you have no idea what they are talking about. He definitely thought I was requesting an entire training course for my one special snowflake. I left it there and passed him the social worker's business card. He tap-tap-tapped the card's edge on the table, then looked at his watch. "OK, are we all set then?"

I WENT HOME AND WROTE an email to Lauren. "I feel like I'm inventing everything as I go and I have to be the expert on all this—with the pediatrician, the preschool teacher, now with the principal. They're supposed to be the experts on kids, but none of them seem to know anything about a kid like mine."

Lauren and I had started to correspond pretty regularly. She told me about her life, about how she had moved alone from the Midwest to San Francisco in her twenties, forty years ago, to take the initial steps to realize her womanhood. I told her about my daughter: her interests and friendships, the cute things she said and did. I also worried openly. I confessed more to Lauren than I did to just about anyone; my friends with cisgender kids couldn't relate, my mom got too upset about her grandchild, and I didn't want to add to the already weighty worries of other parents of trans kids. I definitely didn't want one of the few blogs on the internet about parenting a transgender child to be full of fear and self-doubt.

Lauren would write back with the perfect mix of honesty and optimism:

> I can only imagine how nerve-wracking it must be for you, parenting a young transgender child going through school. Children can be so darned cruel. I myself was bullied and called queer, sissy, and girly. Of course, the last insult was true, because I was a girl!
>
> How lucky M. is to be able to attend kindergarten as the girl she is! What a courageous girl she is to live as herself at such a young age. Perhaps I might have had that kind of courage, but back in the mid-fifties in Nebraska it would have been like saying you were from Mars. My goodness, I wonder how different my life would have turned out. Not that I have any complaints now, of course. Life is grand!

Hearing from Lauren calmed me. She was notably normal. She was from Nebraska and used wholesome phrases like "my goodness." She wrote to me about shifts in the local weather and her home improvement projects and working out at the Y to keep fit. She was a longtime employee of the federal government. She was looking forward to retiring soon, at which point she was thinking about finally cutting her hair short, after all these years. She was even planning a trip to Disneyland.

The fact that she existed at all intrigued and heartened me to no end. Maybe that's how she felt about us, too. I don't know how else to explain such an immediate intimacy with someone I had never laid eyes on.

Lauren answered all of my questions, often before I had asked them, about her childhood and her transition and her life with the man who had loved her for more than forty years. She always apologized for going on too long. "There is just so much to say . . . so much to share," she wrote. "I do hope I'm not boring you with all these stories." But I was far from bored by Lauren from Nebraska, despite her outwardly conventional life. I merely marveled at my luck at being the recipient of her stories.

❖

KINDERGARTEN WAS STARTING in less than a week, and I still hadn't spoken with my child about what we would say to people at her new school. We were walking home from the park when I resolved to do so.

"So, at your new school—" I began.

"I'm kind of scared," she said.

"Scared? Why?"

"Don't know. Just scared."

I said it made sense to be scared when we started something new, like a new school or new job. "I get scared, too." I said. This conversation wasn't going how I'd hoped. How was I going to bring this up without making her even more scared?

"I have to pee!" she said. "Now!"

"Can't you wait til we get home?"

"No!"

She raced onto the grassy parking strip, hoisted up the front of her skirt, and began peeing against a tree, like she'd seen her older male cousins do when we walked with them in the woods near their house. But we lived in the city. I glanced around to see if anyone was watching us.

"Look, Mama!" She giggled. "I'm going to draw a pee heart on this tree!"

Dark splatters appeared on the bark. Not quite a heart, but a circle . . . almost. "I bet *you* wish you could do this, Mama," she shouted over her shoulder. "But you *can't* cuz you have a vagina! Ha ha!"

"Darn it! That's so true! You lucky duck!"

When she was done taunting me for my lack of a penis, I tried again. "You know, some people don't understand that girls can have penises."

"I know that! Like Jack." She stuck out her tongue.

"And there may be some people like Jack at your new school. People who haven't met a girl with a penis before."

She wrinkled up her forehead and considered it. "I'll just explain to them," she said.

"*All* of them or . . . just your close new friends?"

"I'll find the good ones," she said. "And then I'll explain to them."

AT THE END of the first day of school, I stood in the same hallway with the same set of anxious parents, pacing and taking turns stealing peeks through the window of the classroom door. The other parents looked like me, or like people I might be friends with. A lot of us appeared to have gotten into the parenting game a little on the late side. We were dressed for yoga class, or had come straight from the office, or held a younger child in our arms. Mostly moms, plus a few dads. Some of them smiled tentatively at me, and as I smiled back and tried to think of something to say, I realized how different everything was now.

*I look like you*, I thought. *But I am not like you. And my daughter looks like your daughters, but she isn't like them either. When you learn this, will you still smile at me?*

For more than forty years, I had walked into new rooms and expected a warm welcome. I'm white, able-bodied, well educated, employed. That privilege had sat smugly in my lap, ignored and unappreciated until now. You don't notice being warm until you are cold, and then you realize, or you should, how many other people have been cold all along. I still lived near the top of the food chain, but I had lost my swagger.

Blessedly, somehow my child thus far had not. The classroom door flew open, and children poured out of it. My daughter who peed hearts on trees was the first one through it. She was beaming.

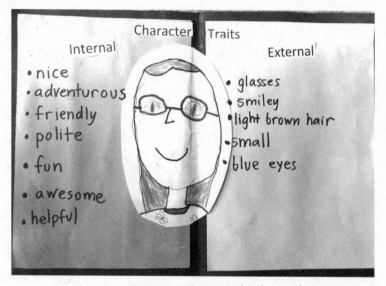

Character Traits

Internal

- nice
- adventurous
- friendly
- polite
- fun
- awesome
- helpful

External

- glasses
- smiley
- light brown hair
- small
- blue eyes

My daughter's self-portrait, age six

# Believe in love.

M om called to see how kindergarten was going. I put her on speaker and held the phone out to my daughter. "How is school, sweetheart?" Grandma said.

"I love it, and Sophie is my best friend," she told her grandma. I had just met Sophie. Alice had had an early meeting on Monday, so I drove the morning carpool. When we walked into the classroom, there was a cluster of kids and parents gathered around an easel with a large piece of white paper clipped to it. In the center of the group, a small, powerful blond presence was hunched over, her nose inches from the paper, scribbling furiously.

"Shall we see what they're up to?" I asked.

"Oh, that's the Morning Question, Mama." M. shrugged. "We have to answer it."

We went closer to investigate. At the top of the easel it said, "What did you do this weekend?" The blond scribbler spun around, brandishing a dangerously uncapped red Sharpie pen. I noticed that she was a leftie, like me. There was red ink smeared across her cheek and a black dot on her chin. Behind her was a black ink drawing of a person apparently tumbling down a set of stairs. She spotted my daughter and shouted to her. "Look! My little sister fell down the stairs this weekend!" I noticed the red lines erupting dramatically from the falling person's head. "That's the blood!" She pointed with the uncapped red pen and cackled.

M. squealed in delighted disgust. The little girl grabbed her hand and pulled her away. "Let's go tell everybody!"

A man standing nearby chuckled self-consciously. "She's the only leftie in the family," he said. "We're not really sure where that came from. We're not really sure where a lot of Sophie's traits came from, actually."

"I can relate to that," I said.

WE INVITED SOPHIE OVER for a playdate. Then they invited M. to their house for another playdate. We got an invitation to Sophie's birthday party. The girls seemed to be inseparable at school. All M.'s stories were Sophie-centered. "I'm so glad you have such a good friend," I told my daughter. And I *was* glad—and also increasingly nervous. M. asked me to invite Sophie over for another playdate, and I heard myself make an excuse to delay.

What were the rules here? How many playdates can you book without telling the parents? Or did you wait until they just found out on their own? Because they probably would. Girls their age were obsessed with dress-up, and I'd seen how quickly and thoughtlessly clothes came off in order to don princess gowns and fairy robes. My daughter often forgot to close the door when she raced off to use the bathroom, and I noticed that Sophie did the same thing when she came to play at our house.

But I struggled with the ethics. Did the other parents have a right to know? Or was this trumped by my daughter's right to privacy? And was that right in turn trumped by concerns about her safety? Before I could answer these questions, it turned out that, once again, my daughter had already handled it.

The kindergarten teacher pulled me aside after school and said, "Sophie's parents asked about M.'s gender." Apparently they had become suspicious when Sophie corrected her dad, who is a neurologist, about anatomy. I cringed, but the teacher laughed. "He's a medical doctor, but apparently he didn't know that girls could have penises, so she set him straight!" I had no problem imagining Sophie doing that.

"But was he . . . OK with it?" I asked.

"Oh, yeah, yeah, totally," the teacher said.

I wondered how long Sophie had known. And how she found out. And why her parents had asked the teacher instead of me.

"Do any of the other kids know?"

"I don't think so," she said. "Sophie is very protective of M. I think it's their special secret."

❖

IN ADDITION TO HER loyal best friend, my daughter had another special new person in her life.

I got my first glimpse of M.'s kindergarten crush one day when I was picking her up from school. The two young lovebirds were skipping across the bark-chipped playground holding hands.

And my daughter wasn't the only one with a new man in her life. I had found myself a boyfriend, too: John, who was clever and fun and gave me a nice giddy feeling when we were together.

I think my daughter felt the same about her little love. I had to drag her off the playground after school. I shared an embarrassed laugh with the little boy's mom when our children embraced and begged us for more time. "I guess it must be almost springtime," I said. "Love is in the air, right?"

She smiled at me. "They're adorable."

About a month into my own romance, on a surprisingly warm spring night, I found myself sitting with John on the rooftop deck of his fancy condo building. The city lights twinkled all around, and a bottle of red wine was disappearing on the table

> **Me:** Can you tell me about your romance with Harry?
>
> **M. (age five):** He said I was pretty, and I said he was handsome. And we held hands like this, and we fell and then we scooted over and kissed.
>
> **Me:** You kissed?
>
> **M.:** Yeah, we did.
>
> **Me:** What does it feel like to be in love?
>
> **M.:** You wanna kiss them. And you wanna marry them!

between us. Our ankles were entwined. I was telling him about my plans to volunteer again for the Trans Pride march. I suggested he attend with me.

I'd already told him about my daughter being transgender, and he'd been cool about it. But as we sipped our wine, and I kept talking about the Pride march, and then about my correspondence with Lauren, his expression changed. "You're so *into* this transgender thing," he said.

He disentangled his ankles from mine. And then he said, "It's your *daughter* who's transgender, right?" John put his wine glass down and looked me over really carefully, with an intensity that was not at all romantic.

I reassured him: Yes, I was talking about my daughter, *not* about me.

*Definitely not about me.*

*What a crazy idea! Of course not.*

John looked relieved. He relaxed and leaned back into me and smiled, and we changed the subject and finished the bottle of wine.

I didn't tell a soul about my conversation with John. I think I was too ashamed. But I couldn't stop thinking about it. I had not lied to John. But I had not been brave, either. I had been so quick to reassure him that I was not transgender, so desperate to make sure that he didn't think I was . . . like her. I felt like I'd just sold out my own child. I wondered: What would it be like, on nights like these, for my daughter? Would she lie to guys like John? Would she be like me and tell them what they wanted to hear in order to be loved? Or would she be braver than her mother had been? And would they still love her when they learned that she *was* transgender?

What would little Harry's mom say when she learned this detail about her son's first love? Would she still find their kindergarten romance so adorable? A couple of weeks later, John broke up with me. He said he met someone else.

I logged back on to the dating website to give it another try. I clicked through profiles for what felt like ages, but nobody looked right for me. Then I found someone who seemed promising. I was about to send him a message when I read the last line of his profile. It said, *No trannies, please.*

---

**Me:** What happened to your romance with Harry?

**M.:** Well, it was too much, playing every single day together at recess. I told him that I wanted space. I said we could just play on Fridays, but not all the other days.

**Me:** That sounds like a good plan.

**M.:** It was. But then, it felt like he did space without telling me!

**Me:** He stopped playing with you but didn't tell you?

**M.:** Yeah. So, I asked him if he still loved me, and he said no. It felt like my heart broke.

**Me:** Sometimes love is difficult.

**M.:** It doesn't always stay.

Dear Marlo,

I thought I would write to you the day after my marriage!!
As you know, Thomas and I have been together for over
35 years. As we approach retirement, we decided it was
important to take a step to secure our future. We got married
at City Hall. The ceremony was brief, but the judge was
so sweet. We both dressed up, Thomas in his pinstriped
dark blue suit and me in a gold silk pant suit and pearls.
We went out to an early dinner and then came home and
had champagne in chilled glasses. It wasn't a storybook
wedding, but it really does sort of put the frosting on the
cake. I still can't believe that I am an old married woman
now! It is what I dreamed of back when I was 16 years old.

Love to you and M.,
Lauren


PS: I am confident that you will meet a great guy one of
these days soon who will treasure you the way you deserve.
It always seems to happen when you least expect it, so don't
try chasing after it too hard.

❖

ON MY DAUGHTER'S SIXTH BIRTHDAY, my family came over for dinner. The cake was pink and so were most of her presents. Everyone was calling her M. now, except for the occasional lapse. Dad
had used her boy name once while we were clearing up after

dinner. My sister gave me a nervous look, but no one else seemed to have noticed and M. was busy in another room playing with her cousins. I let it pass.

The kids stormed into the living room. M. raised her arms above her head and called out, "Ladies and gentlemen! Ladies and gentlemen! Please take your seats!"

My sister and I obediently joined Grandma and Auntie S. on the couch. Grandpa made the rounds with a wine bottle, refilling glasses. My daughter was impatient. "The show is starting! Take your seats! Grandpa, that means *you!*"

The show turned out to be a gripping medical drama. M. was the star and apparently also the director. She stood in front of the fireplace with a plastic baby doll stuffed into her dress, clutching her sides and moaning in apparent agony. She shouted at her cousin, who stood nearby. "Husband! Husband! Catch the baby! Catch the baby!" Her cousin took a couple of reluctant steps toward her, looking at his feet, clearly regretting his decision to participate in this performance.

"Hurry!" his young wife shouted again. "The baby is coming!" But he was too late. The doll dropped to the ground with a thud. M. huffed and stomped a foot. "Again! We need to do it again!"

The moaning recommenced, and this time the seven-year-old husband dutifully snatched his newborn baby as it escaped from his wife's shirt. He stuffed it under his arm.

We all recognized the story. My parents' goddaughter had just given birth while standing up in the hospital waiting room, and her husband had actually caught their baby before the doctors showed up to help. I'm assuming *he* caught it on the first try.

The living room audience cheered and the children bowed and I marveled silently at the cruel irony of this scene, of watching my child act out a role that she would never play. She didn't have a womb, and the hormones she'd need to take to be viewed as a woman would render her infertile. And I was fairly certain that she had no idea.

My daughter grabbed the baby from her cousin. "The baby's hungry!" she said. "It needs milk!" She mashed the doll's face into her chest.

"You are such a good mommy!" Grandma said.

The little mother grinned. "I know."

"Show's over," my nephew said.

I ALWAYS WANTED TO BE a mother. And I never doubted I would be.

I was lucky. Like the other women in my family, I had no problem getting pregnant and then had an easy pregnancy, a straightforward delivery, and a beautiful, healthy baby.

I always assumed I'd be a grandmother one day, too. But now, with my child still in kindergarten, I was coming to terms with the fact that I would never be one. At least not a biological one, not in the "she has your eyes" kind of way, like my own mother is to her three grandchildren.

I kept trying to think of ways to explain all this to my daughter. I wanted to be the one to tell her. I wanted to be there when she learned about this loss so I could answer her questions if it confused her, and comfort her if it made her sad. I wanted to reassure her that there were other ways to become a parent.

How do you tell a young child that one of the things most people assume they'll be able to do one day is probably off the table for her?

Once again, we were in the car driving somewhere when she told me she already knew, or nearly knew. From the back seat, out of the blue, I heard her say, "People with vaginas have babies." And then, "So because I don't have a vagina I can't have a baby."

I pulled over, turned off the engine, and spun around. "How long have you known that?"

"In order to have a baby, I'd need to be gay," she said. "I have to marry another girl."

"I didn't realize you were thinking about this," I said.

"Yeah, cuz I'd make the sperm, but she'd need to make the egg."

So she understood, but not completely. And now it was my job to finish off the last hope she had. "Right, the thing is, honey, if you want to take the medicine to be a woman when you grow up, then you can't have . . . your sperm won't work. Probably."

"You mean I won't have a baby," she said.

I rushed to explain that she could always adopt, and that adopting was also a real and wonderful way to become a mother. I said that there *might* be a way for her to have a baby, that doctors and scientists were working on it, trying to figure out new ways for people like her to have their own kids. And it was true. I had heard of some experimental treatments that could, maybe, allow her to be a biological parent. They'd had some success in the lab, with mice. But it sounded like science fiction, and practically speaking, it might as well be.

So I said, "No, you probably won't be able to have your own baby, sweetheart."

**Me:** Wow, you have a lot of stuffed animals on your bed. You gonna kiss all of them good night?

**M. (age five):** I'll try.

**Me:** Are you their mom?

**M.:** I consider them my babies. Each morning I give them like maybe three or two kisses each, so if they're patient and don't scream with impatientness, then they win an award, like an extra five kisses in the afternoon or morning.

**Me:** You seem like a very good mother.

**M.:** Yes. I told them rules, told them boundaries, put them at their best behavior.

**Me:** You're a pretty strict parent.

**M.:** Well, I like to keep my babies safe.

**Me:** That's important. What are their names?

**M.:** Oh, dear, I can't actually remember. Sometimes I make it up. I feel horrible. I just wanna give them name tags but that will take forever.

**Me:** Well, you do have a lot of babies.

M. with her favorite doll

❖

WE WERE GETTING READY for school, and her favorite dress was in the wash. She fished around in the back of a drawer and pulled out a pair of jeans that had been handed down to her. "I'll wear these," she said.

"Are you sure?" My child had not worn jeans, nor pants of any variety, for three full years.

"Yup," she said, pulling them on. "They fit just right!"

We had recently wrapped up the first Halloween in which she had not been either a princess or a fairy. Instead, she had wanted to be Pippi Longstocking. Pippi *is* a girl—the strongest girl in the world, in fact. Pippi could lift a horse, but she was certainly no princess.

My daughter told me that she didn't like princesses anymore. I was shocked and asked for clarification. "But *why?*"

"I don't know," she said. "They're just kind of dumb."

I could not argue with this. As a feminist, I should have been relieved at the departure of the Disney princess from my daughter's imagination. But instead, I was troubled. Princesses had been replaced by Pokémon, a passion she shared with her new friend at school, a *boy*. "I love sword fighting," she said one day. "I'm the best sword fighter at school." And now, after three years of a strict no-pants policy, pants were back on the menu.

I confided in Alice. "What if this means she really isn't a girl?" I said. "What if she's trying to tell me she has changed her mind?"

"Oh, Mama," Alice said. "Your kitty cat sure is keeping you on your toes!"

I tried to picture doing everything again, in reverse: telling family, neighbors, the school, that the girl who was a boy is a boy again. We take it back. Never mind. It would be confusing, but ultimately, easier. I knew that some people would be relieved or feel vindicated when our gender-switching experiment finally failed.

"It would be OK," I said.

"Oh, Marlo," Alice squeezed my arm. "You'd miss her."

"I would . . . I already said goodbye once to my son. I don't want to have to say goodbye to my daughter now."

"But you will, if you have to."

That night I sat my daughter down and told her I needed her to listen to me carefully. I said that some people decide to change their gender more than once, and some people do it when they're seven or seventeen. Or even forty-two, like Mama. "I can change my gender to being a boy if I want to."

"Or nonbinary," said M. "You can be a *they* if you want."

"What?"

"Like Conner from camp last summer. Conner was a *they.*"

"Oh! Exactly. So, if you change your mind, and decide that *you* are a *they* or a *he*, that's OK. You're still the same person, and your dad and I will always love you, no matter what gender you are."

My child patted my hand gently and looked at me like I wasn't very smart. "Look, Mama, *most* people who love sword fighting are boys. But I'm a *girl* who really loves sword fighting." I had not mentioned sword fighting, Pokémon, or pants. But she knew. She knew why her mother was having doubts, and she also knew what I should have known: that none of these things had anything to do with whether you were a girl or not.

"That's right. You're absolutely right. You're strong *and* you're a girl. Like Pippi Longstocking."

"Yes. She's the strongest girl in the world. Did you know that she can lift a horse?"

❖

I HAD BEEN MAKING short audio recordings of my child since she was born. Sometimes I used a cheap recorder I had bought, but mostly I just used my iPhone. At first, I made these recordings just for myself, just so I could hang on to the sound of her sweet little voice, wanting to preserve more of her small self for later. Like all parents do.

By early 2014, when she had just turned six years old, podcasts were starting to become a big thing. It occurred to me that I could try to make one using my growing collection of recordings. Since a podcast would only be audio, I figured I could still keep us anonymous, but also possibly reach more people than I did with my blog. I also thought a podcast might make us seem more "real," if people could actually hear my child's voice—and mine.

I decided to call it *How to Be a Girl*, and I began with a short episode that told our whole story up to that point in just over seven minutes. I spliced in conversations between me and my daughter. Some of these conversations were serious, like when she told me she was angry that I had mistaken her for a boy. Some were just fun and silly. I wanted people to understand that we were "normal." I wanted them to see that we were, in all the ways that really mattered, just like everybody else.

> **Me:** Can you tell our listeners a little bit about yourself?
>
> **M. (age six):** My name is M. My favorite color is blue, my favorite animal is birds, and I like to hang out with the people I love.

The logo for my new podcast

**Me:** What is it like to be a girl?

**M. (age six):** It feels good, because I wanted to be one.

**Me:** Do you remember when your papa and I said, "No, you're a boy. You can be a boy who likes pink"?

**M.:** Yeah. And that was really upsetting. I forgive you.

Over the next few years, I produced a series of podcast episodes on no particular schedule and with no particular plan other than to give people some idea of what it was like to be raising a child I had never expected to raise. I openly confessed all my worries and fears and self-doubt, and I placed my daughter in front of the microphone to let her have her say.

I drew some simple pictures to accompany a few of the episodes and then created cartoons that I posted on YouTube. I wanted people to be able to hear our story even if they didn't know how to listen to a podcast.

After I'd made several episodes, I asked my ex if he'd be willing to be on the podcast with me. Things were a lot better between us. We had never sat down and hashed everything out, nor said sorry for the mean things we'd both said and done, but we'd been forced to work together, sorting out schools and meeting doctors and psychologists, and over time we became a team again—but in a new way.

As we sat down to record our conversation, it dawned on me that I had never actually heard his version of this story. I had never heard how he came to accept having a daughter rather than a son.

So I asked him.

Will said that after our "son" had told him she was actually a girl, he had stalled, like I did, hoping the phase would pass. Like me, he was terrified about what it might mean if our child really were transgender. "I wanted to leave the door open for our kid to have the easiest life possible. And in my mind, the easiest life possible was to live as one's biological gender."

Everything changed for him one evening, when he attended one of the support group meetings at the Children's Hospital. He said he had looked around the room and realized that the parents there were divided into two groups: the fearful ones and the calm ones. Like him, most of the fearful parents were new to the group, "and we were just swimming in agony." The calm ones had been coming to the group for months, some of them for years. Will's voice began to quiver. "And they spoke about their kids with joy and love."

"And their kids were doing OK, right?" I asked.

He took a long slow breath. "They weren't going to die," my child's father said. "Part of me thought my kid was going to die because she was transgender."

After the meeting, he said, he went straight home and got down on his knees so he could be eye to eye with our child. "You get to decide," he told her. "I don't get to decide."

And our child looked into his eyes and relaxed, transforming before him, "like the opening of a flower." And from that moment on, their whole relationship changed. "Before, everything was tense and contested, everything was a fight. Afterward, we were at peace."

I blinked back tears. So did he. "So, from that day, you switched pronouns and—"

"And that was it. Never looked back once. Never had a moment of doubt that we were doing the right thing."

# Find a role model.

Lauren emailed me a photo of herself as a young woman, newly transitioned. Her hair falls just below her shoulders. She's wearing huge brown seventies glasses and a peasant blouse, and it looks like she's at a party. She is barefoot, sitting on the floor, like young people do at parties, and her close-lipped smile is smug and cool as she stares right into the camera. She looks content. "I was so excited when I got my first job as a waitress," she wrote. "It was a tough time, but I was absolutely fearless."

**Me:** What do you think it's gonna be like to be a grown-up transgender woman?

**M. (age seven):** Special.

**Me:** Why?

**M.:** I don't know.

Lauren was enrolled in Stanford University's Gender Dysphoria Program, where a psychiatric evaluation was followed by a two-year "real-life test," to prove you could "pass"—and make a living—in your "chosen" gender, before doctors would sign off on surgeries. She was on her own in a new, strange city, and no one back home in Nebraska knew what she was up to, not her widowed mother, nor her four younger brothers. "For me, the goal was everything," she wrote. "I would have endured anything to reach my goal."

I wrote back and said that I thought she was incredibly courageous.

"That is very kind of you to say," she replied. "But I don't think I'm courageous. I simply did what I had to do. I can't even imagine what kind of courage it would have required from me to try to live my life as a male."

"Well, I still think you're amazing," I responded. "And speaking of amazing, did you see Laverne Cox on the cover of *Time* magazine?"

IT WAS ALL OVER social media. And there was a text from Alice full of exclamation points: "Laverne is a goddess!!"

On June 9, 2014, the cover of *Time* magazine had announced a TRANSGENDER TIPPING POINT: AMERICA'S NEXT CIVIL RIGHTS FRONTIER. Next to the exciting headline, posing elegantly in black heels and a figure-hugging blue dress, was transgender actress Laverne Cox, a star on the hit Netflix show *Orange Is the New Black*.

Was it true? Was the world finally going to offer people like my child a permanent seat at the table? Or would this all fade away in the next news cycle, as it had done so many times before? I was cautiously hopeful. Maybe *this* time we wouldn't forget about them and go back to pretending they didn't exist.

I bought a fat stack of copies of *Time*'s "tipping point" issue to share with family and friends, and to save for posterity. M. scanned the glossy cover, took in the glamorous lady, and said, "Who is she?" I said she was a very famous actress, who was smart and talented.

"Huh," she said. "Pretty dress."

"And also, she's . . . when she was born, they thought she was a boy. Like you."

"That's cool."

"Yeah, it is. It's cool."

I had been so excited to share this moment with her, but now I was at a loss for words. How could I share the good news without also sharing the bad? *Someone like you has never been on the cover of a major magazine before. The magazine says that people like you might finally have rights soon. Maybe.* I could not bring myself to say these things to my six-year-old.

How do you dole out the news to a young child that her identity has landed her far down on society's pecking order? How do you explain that she is part of a group that *needs* a civil rights movement because people like her currently possess almost no legal rights? It was also true that my daughter possessed piles of privilege, as a white US citizen born to parents with college degrees and good jobs. I decided that what was needed was context—and hope.

"Remember Martin Luther King?" I said.

She nodded.

"One-hundred-fifty years ago in this country, Black people were slaves," I said. "When my grandmother was born, women weren't allowed to vote, and when I was your age, no one I knew had two mommies or two daddies." This last fact seemed to shock her. Half the kids in kindergarten had two mommies. *"Really?* Why not?"

"Because people thought gay people were . . ."

"Bad?"

"Yes, bad."

My child scowled and crossed her arms. "I like Rory's mommies," she said.

"Me, too. So that's why people keep fighting to change things in order to give everyone equal rights. People like Martin Luther King Jr. fought so that Black people would be treated better. Women fought to get the right to vote. And gay people are still fighting for the right to get married. And transgender people—"

"Wait, Rory's mommies can't get *married?!*"

"And today, some people think that it's not OK to be a girl with a penis, to be transgender." I pointed to Laverne. "And this woman, she is fighting to tell everyone that transgender people are the same as everyone else. She's like Martin Luther King Jr. And she's like you."

My child set her pointer finger on the magazine and dragged it slowly across the headline. "T . . . trrrrrr . . . trrrraaaannnzzz

. . . tranzzzz . . . gender! Transgender!"

After that we started using the word *transgender*, phasing out "girl with a penis." I thought it was time.

WHEN I TOLD HER that we'd soon be going once again to a conference where everyone was transgender, or had a family member who was transgender, she did a double take. Apparently this amazing fact had escaped her last year. "Really? *Everybody?*"

"Yep."

She squealed and started jumping up and down. "Can we go right now?"

The conference was still two months away, so I suggested we try to find some transgender kids to play with sooner.

"But how will we ever find them, Mama?"

"We'll order them on the magical internet!" I said, and we giggled and I logged onto our support group discussion list to place our order. We wrote it together:

*We are seeking a transgender girl, age six or seven, to come for a playdate. Preferably one who likes fairies AND sword fighting.*

A reply came that very day: "Matthew is seven and she *loves* both fairies and sword fighting. We're really new to this, but we'd love to come for a playdate."

That weekend, Matthew and her mother, Margaret, appeared at our door. "Sorry we're late," Margaret said. "I hadn't realized how far it was." She had driven almost two hours to find someone like Matthew. M. grabbed Matthew by the hand and suggested they go outside to play with her fairy garden.

Margaret and I drank tea and spied on them through the kitchen window. Two little girls in sundresses bent over the collection of plastic fairies and other treasures in a weedy flower bed. One of the girls seemed to be doing most of the talking. The other girl had very short hair.

"We only transitioned a few months ago," Margaret said. "She hasn't wanted to change her name, which is kind of confusing for people. Maybe meeting your daughter will help."

"Maybe," I said, struck by the notion of my child serving as a role model at age six.

"Your daughter seems so confident," Margaret said. "How did you accomplish that?"

"I don't know. I think she was born that way," I said, which felt true.

After they left, I asked M. if she'd had fun with her new friend.

"It was wonderful and perfect," she said.

"I'm so glad," I began to say, but she wasn't finished.

"Because now I know there is someone else on Earth who is like me."

❖

THERE SEEMED TO BE a lot more families at the conference that summer. Maybe I imagined it, but the vibe felt different, too: more confident and defiant. It had felt that way at the second Trans Pride march in June, our numbers greater, our chants fiercer. Maybe the "tipping point" was a real thing.

My child seemed to have tipped into a new reality, too. Maybe it was being six years old, not five or four. Maybe it was Laverne and my awkward history speech on civil rights. Maybe it was Matthew. Maybe it was all of this. But the net effect was a new self-consciousness about what made her different, tinged with pride but also with fear.

She asked me to take down all the old photos that made her look like a boy, including my favorite, the blue-eyed baby photo she used to look at and just see herself. Now, I guess she saw the baby boy I saw. "I don't want anyone to see that picture," she said. She asked if I'd let her change to a school where all the kids were transgender. She was shocked and angry when I told her no such school existed.

Skirts came back, and pants were once again banned, but not for fashion this time, not to make a point about being a real girl. This time, skirts were necessary to conceal. I asked her about the return of skirts.

"I'm afraid someone's gonna see my penis and think it's funny."

"Did anyone ever tease you about this?"

"No," she said. "Doesn't mean it won't happen."

I couldn't argue with that. I told her I'd heard that you could buy special underpants. "For girls like you. They hold things in a bit, and they're more comfortable if you have a penis."

"Please buy them, Mama," she begged.

I found them online. Each pair was custom-made and cost over twenty dollars. I ordered three.

She loved them. I felt guilty for not buying them sooner. I ordered six more.

"You know you're beautiful, right?" I said. "Your body is beautiful and perfect." I had never warmed to the phrase "born in the wrong body," and I had avoided using it with her. "The wrong body" according to whom? Why couldn't she love her body just as it was? Perhaps her penis did feel misplaced, and she'd take care of that one day. Or perhaps it only felt wrong because everyone else said it should. I refused to join that chorus.

But I couldn't deny that her body marked her out as different, in everyone else's eyes and now apparently in her own, too. At the conference that summer, the same doctor who had told us about blockers the previous year gave us parents a stern warning about the dangers of pretending our kids were like everyone else. She said it was all well and good to be "uber-accepting" of our children, but we had to find a way to help them incorporate the "transgender" part of themselves into their identity. "Your kids are not cisgender," she said, "and they never will be."

"I'm definitely only going to marry boys when I'm grown up," my daughter told me one day, out of the blue.

"OK. But if you change your mind, you can marry a girl if you want."

She shook her head and was quiet for a moment. I watched her search for the right words. "I'm not against gay," she said finally. "But being gay is less usual. And I'm *already* transgender."

"So . . . you don't want to be gay because . . . it would make you even more different?"

"Yeah."

❖

Hi gendermom. I'm 22 years old and I'm trans too
(specifically, nonbinary, gender-fluid, genderqueer). I just
told my family. My mother refuses to discuss it. My dad thinks
it's just a phase and I'll grow out of it. But I know they are
wrong. I've had horrible depressions and break-downs my
whole life, until I finally realized what was wrong. I can't go
back now.

ON THE FIRST DAY of the conference, a boyish young man came up
to me and introduced himself. "Any chance you're gendermom?"

"How did you know?"

"Lucky guess. I follow your blog. I'm Micah."

Except Micah wasn't a young man. Micah was nonbinary and
used they/them pronouns. They told me they were at the conference to lead a session on nonbinary transition. I had no idea
what that was.

My daughter tugged my arm. We were late for camp. "Meet for
lunch?" Micah said.

"Who was that guy?" she asked.

"They are Micah."

I could feel my brain pushing back against this new pronoun.
A plural where it wanted to put a singular, an apparent blank
where it wanted to insert either male or female. I was skeptical.
I was finally beginning to wrap my head around the notion of
switching genders, of toggling between the only two options I
had ever heard of. But *another* gender that was neither just male
nor just female? Was this really a real thing?

I learned that Micah had a blog, too. Before we met for lunch, I started reading it.

"Since 2010 I've been transitioning—or rather, trying to figure out what transition means to me, as someone whose gender is neither female nor male." Micah called themselves "neutral gendered." They were born female, they said, but couldn't bear being seen as a woman. "Every time I hear a *she* or *miss*," Micah wrote, "ice caps melt."

"Being a female means I was granted not one, but *two* small-medium-size-ish round thingies where my chest should be. This has been effectively remedied." Micah wrote openly about something called "top surgery" to have their breasts removed, and about taking low doses of testosterone to appear slightly more masculine without going so far as to grow a beard. They also didn't wish to be seen as a man. "I wish my body to be as neutral as possible."

I thought about the mother I'd witnessed in a recent support group meeting. She was crying, like all the new moms did, and saying the same heartbreaking things: Her child wanted to disappear. Her child couldn't bear hearing the feminine name and pronouns she'd had since birth. But her child wasn't a boy either. Her child claimed to be something else, and not being seen as that something else was apparently as intolerable for her child as it was for my child to be seen as a boy. This was another kind of unicorn, and it was real, too.

Lunch with Micah was like lunch with an old friend. We had the same sense of humor. We talked about my daughter and about our families and the books we were reading. By the end of our lunch, I had forgotten that Micah had a gender I didn't believe in just a few hours ago. Micah was Micah. They were them. They made sense. I didn't need to put Micah in one box or the other, something I couldn't have imagined could ever work, let alone be so easy. Micah was another person. A person I really liked.

For the first time, I considered my own gender. I had never questioned nor been troubled by my identity as a woman, but what about me actually felt "like a girl?" I liked dopey rom-coms and historical costume dramas. I liked a lot of daintily patterned things—flowers and pretty tablecloths and French braids. I could spend an eternity talking with my girlfriends about our relationships and our feelings, but I also related to men well as friends. I often felt more left-brained than right. Like my daughter, I dug sword fighting. I hated shopping. I spent zero time on my hair in the morning. And, much to my daughter's chagrin, I hated dresses. I never wore them. When I thought of donning a flowy floral-print sundress, I felt like I was playing dress-up as someone else. Like I wasn't even me. I had no idea why, but it was just like that and had been for as long as I could remember. Was that what it had been like for my daughter when we made her dress like a boy? It must have been.

I knew wearing sundresses didn't make you a girl, of course. But then, what did? And did I really feel that I was completely and totally 100 percent "girl?" Or might I be just a little bit "boy," too? Suddenly my own gender seemed more complicated and interesting than I had ever considered. Maybe this was true for everyone.

The support group facilitator had often said that gender was really more like a spectrum, or even a web or a constellation. And rather than just two poles, we were all finding our unique spot in a gender universe. This made sense to me now. Maybe there were as many genders as there are people on the planet. Wow.

I felt sheepish for thinking only people like my daughter had an interesting gender. Everybody did. It was just that the people who played the gender game within the two traditional boxes got to tell themselves that their genders weren't as complex and arbitrary as someone like my daughter or Micah, or me. But I was onto them now.

Things got even more complicated when I followed a link from Micah's blog to a series of websites about something called "intersex" conditions. These were cases where biological sex didn't align with the neat gender binary either. These were things I'd never learned about in health class: people who appeared to be female but had XY chromosomes, people born with ambiguous genitalia, or with hormone levels that resulted in reproductive systems that could not be easily classified as either male or female. And these conditions aren't as rare as you might think. Nearly 2 percent of us are born with some form of intersex condition. That was more common than redheads. It wasn't just gender that lived on a spectrum. Biological sex did, too.

Nothing was as it had seemed.

---

"Gender is not sane. It's not sane to call a rainbow black and white."
—Kate Bornstein, *Gender Outlaw: On Men,*
*Women and the Rest of Us*

---

❖

FIRST GRADE STARTED, and M. learned to read. Sophie was in her class again and was still her best friend—still the lone keeper of my daughter's secret.

I kept thinking about M.'s request for an all-transgender school and about what she said after her playdate with Matthew. No one should feel that alone on the earth. We still went to the support group, but it only met once a month and often none of the kids who showed up were her age. Or worse, they were mostly boys.

"What if we created a play group just for kids like you? A special club of only transgender kids."

"Yessss!!!! We will call it 'The Ninja Girls Play Group'!"

I said we might want to have a name that includes boys and nonbinary kids, too. And maybe the group name should include the word *transgender?*

"Nope. We'll call it 'The Be-Your-True-Self Play Group.'"

> **Me:** What's it feel like when you meet other transgender kids?
>
> **M. (age seven):** I feel less alone in the world.

A FEW WEEKS LATER, my daughter and I watched, with mounting excitement, as small children, clutching parents' hands, appeared in the doorway of the basement playroom at our neighborhood community center for the first meeting of the True Self Play Group. The response to my invitation on our support group discussion list had been enthusiastic and large—much too large to host in our very small house. So I rented the room and asked everyone to chip in a few bucks to cover it.

My daughter struck up an instant friendship with the first girl roughly her size to enter the room. They danced and tumbled on a gymnastics mat in the corner, collapsing over and over again in fits of loud and hysterical laughter. She took the briefest of breaks to fill me in, running up to me, breathless with excitement. "We're almost the same, except for our hair," she said of her brown-headed doppelgänger. "She's transgender *and* she's seven, *and* her parents are divorced! Can you believe it?!" She hugged me and ran back to her friend, and they were soon joined by some late arrivals—two more girls around the same age. I watched in stunned gratitude as they held hands and danced around in a circle.

Three very small children, perhaps four or five years old, crept shyly around the room. Their hair was boyishly short, and they all wore the same gauzy and impractical princess dresses my daughter used to pine for. My invitation had also included a request for some transgender teenagers to come and help out. A couple of fourteen-year-old girls showed up with their mothers and a large collection of nail polishes. They laid out the bottles of polish, one by one, on a low table, and asked if anyone wanted a manicure. One of the short-haired princesses was coaxed into a chair and invited to select a color. Pink, of course. I stood between the mother of the teenage manicurist and the mother of the princess, as the tiny nails were brushed into a pale pink. "This is amazing," both moms said at the same time. Their eyes were moist. So were mine. Two more princesses lined up for their turns.

Only one boy showed up, and he looked glum when he took in the girl-heavy scene. I apologized to his mom. "We'll try and recruit more boys next time."

"There's always more girls at this age," she said. "It makes sense, I guess. If you're a young girl who likes boy stuff, everyone just thinks you have a tomboy."

A light went on in my brain. "Right! But if you're a boy who likes dresses—"

The mom of my daughter's doppelgänger chimed in. "Your parents freak out and call a psychiatrist!"

We shared a rueful laugh.

"There will be more boys later," the boy's mom predicted. "When the kids get older and the parents realize they don't have a tomboy. They have a *boy*."

"WHO WERE THOSE big beautiful girls?" M. asked on the drive home.

"You mean the teenagers who were painting fingernails?" M. had been too busy with her new friends to get herself a manicure, so I wondered if she'd noticed the big girls at all.

"They are teenagers," I said. "Transgender teenagers."

There was only silence from the back seat for the rest of the drive home, but as we climbed out of the car in the driveway, she announced, "I'm glad I'm transgender."

The "big beautiful girls" got me thinking. I remembered how I had idolized my teenaged babysitters when I was a kid. The best of them were the coolest creatures on the planet, and everything they did and said was fascinating and irresistible. I'd look at my reflection in the bathroom mirror and think, *One day I'll be just like Ingrid.* I also thought I'd be like my mother, who was pretty and sweet and had a husband and three children and a lovely home. But who would my daughter be like? Who would *she* see when she gazed in the mirror and imagined herself at seventeen, or heaven forbid, something as ancient as thirty? Who would counsel her along the way? As the doctor at the conference had said, she was not cisgender, and never would be. And I would never be trans. There were limits to what I could teach her.

There was a young transgender man who mentored all the teenagers at the support group. I sent him an email. Did he know of any mature teen girls or young trans women who might want to be a role model, a "big sister" to my little girl? He wrote back and asked, "Have you met Anna?"

I had. Anna had been one of the volunteers watching the kids at the conference day camp that summer. We spoke briefly when I dropped my daughter off at camp. She was young— twenty-something—with a wide, movie-star smile and gorgeous long, dark hair that my daughter would love. She was also memorably warm and sweet. Yes, she would do.

I invited Anna over for dinner. Then we met for brunch. She joined us on Halloween to go trick-or-treating, bringing along her handsome boyfriend. On my daughter's birthday, she showed up with a giant beauty kit for little girls full of nail polish and lip gloss.

Anna had a good job at a bank and a nice apartment downtown. She wanted to have a family someday. M. would climb in her lap and they'd take selfies and play on Anna's phone and shriek with laughter.

"Mama, we did a face swap on Snapchat!"

"On what?"

"Oh, Mama, you're not cool, because you're old."

*This is what I wanted*, I thought. *This is exactly what I wanted.*

After the girls made cookies, I asked Anna to stay for dinner. She looked tired, and I felt maternal. I *was* old enough to be her mom, too. Or at least her big sister.

She said she was worn out and she'd love to stay for dinner. "I had laser yesterday, and girlfriend, let me tell you—it hurts like hell."

"What's 'laser'?" M. asked.

"Oh, little zaps to get rid of hairs." Anna pointed to her chin. "Mine are mostly gone, but I have to get little touch-ups now and then."

"Lasers?" My daughter looked frightened.

"Oh, don't you worry." Anna cupped M.'s chin in her hand and smiled. "This lucky girl won't have to do that. Your life is going to be a lot different than mine, hon."

It was true. Anna had only transitioned two years earlier, at twenty-five. She had been working as a drag queen when she realized she wasn't dressing up as a woman—she *was* a woman.

After she transitioned, she worked at the only job she thought she could get, entertaining a clientele of older men who had a thing for trans girls. She quit when she got a job at the bank and realized that too many of her girlfriends doing that work had, as she put it, "been made into soup or something." She told me she had blocked most of it out.

Her handsome boyfriend was a former client. He had a temper, and sometimes it got "out of hand" and he knocked her around. I was relieved when she broke up with him.

"I don't need that crap anymore. I'm *off* dating now," she said. "I just deleted Tinder."

"What's Tinder?" M. said.

"A place to meet boys," Anna said. "Do *you* like any boys?"

M. made a grossed-out face. "No."

"Good girl." Anna put up her hand and they high-fived. "Boys are stupid. Avoid them at all costs."

THAT NIGHT I STOOD in the bathroom doorway and watched my daughter brush her teeth. I noticed that her pajama pants had gotten even shorter, now barely clearing her knees. Her bedtime T-shirt seemed to have shrunk, too. I examined her thinned-out face, the length of her fingers wrapped around her toothbrush. I wondered what she would look like at seventeen, at thirty. And I wondered who *she* saw in the mirror of her imagination. I wondered how you find a role model for the first of its kind.

"Anna is a lot like you, because you're both awesome and you're both trans," I said. "But she's also different from you."

She spat in the sink and looked at herself in the mirror. "Different how?"

"Well, she lived as a boy when she was your age, and for a while as an adult, too."

"That's sad," said M., frowning at her reflection.

# Question everything.

My daughter was hard at work on her list for Santa, vacillating daily between requesting a LEGO castle or an opulent set of princess gowns, with one for every day of the week.

"Do you think I can ask for both?" she asked, her face alight with a wild, momentary hope, followed by a sudden frown. "Or will that make him mad?"

Her first-grade class was planning a winter celebration that seemed to revolve around masses of hand-cut

> **Me:** What would you say to someone who says, "If you have a penis, you're a boy"?
>
> **M. (age seven):** I would say, "How do you know? It's not a rule!"

snowflakes. I picked little triangular shards of paper out of her hair after school each day.

Lauren checked in with a long email. She had just put up her Christmas tree and was in a philosophical mood.

> I have been thinking deeply on this topic. The transgender condition has existed since the dawn of time, and yet I wonder how people like myself survived in the past. I mean before hormones and surgical intervention. What did they do? I can only assume that they merely suffered through it all and lived miserably unhappy lives or they died early at their own hands or others. I thank God that I was born in a time and place where I could do something about it and find my own happiness and security. What a Russian roulette it all is!

She wanted to know what my daughter had on her list for Santa and whether it was OK for her to mail M. a gift.

> Goodness me, the Christmas season upon us already! But I am not sure how much I like Christmas.

THAT WINTER, LEELAH ALCORN killed herself. She was seventeen when she posted her suicide note on social media and stepped in front of a semitruck on the interstate. "I decided I've had enough," Leelah wrote. When she told her parents she was a girl, they had sent her to conversion therapy to fix her. They told her that God didn't make mistakes, and that she would always be their son. "Please don't tell this to your kids," Leelah wrote.

"That won't do anything but make them hate themself. That's exactly what it did to me."

Leelah's suicide note went viral and made national headlines, along with selfies she had taken posing in the mirror. I could hardly bear to look at them.

Some said her suicide vindicated parents like me. That it proved we were doing the right thing, because at least *our* children were still breathing. They blamed Leelah's parents for her death and said they should be prosecuted for causing it. Some questioned whether they had even loved their child.

I was sure they did love her. I failed to see them as monsters. I did think they were tragically mistaken, but what parent gets it all right? I had stumbled and doubted every step of the way since my own child's first terrifying announcement, and more stumbling and doubting was sure to come. What if we were *all* one decision away from being Leelah's parents? What if we were all one decision away from indescribable loss?

It was easier to make them into monsters.

Parents like me were staking everything on what people were starting to call the "gender affirming" model, allowing our kids to live in the gender they said they were. But there were plenty of people who weren't on board with this model. Leelah's parents would have had no shortage of authority figures telling them that *I* was the one who was mistaken. Those condemning my approach would likely have included not just their pastor but also the school principal and their child's pediatrician, whose opinions would most probably be echoed by a psychologist, if they consulted one. Half the parents in my support group had a story of some medical professional suggesting an approach similar to the one the Alcorns had taken. And they also had the law on their side: At the time, in 2014, conversion therapy—therapy intended to change someone's sexual orientation or gender identity—was completely legal in all but two US states.

Even in my liberal West Coast state, people around me kept citing the dubious and debunked statistic that said 80 percent of kids like mine wouldn't actually end up transgender. Parts of our extended family were making it clear that they thought my child's "girl phase" had gone on long enough and someone should put their foot down.

There was also a name I kept hearing, usually from another parent at the support group, usually spoken with a shudder because, like any proper villain, he was both terrifying and powerful. News stories about kids like mine quoted him. NPR called him "one of the leaders in his field," and he was: He ran a large clinic for transgender youth in Canada and he had led the work group on "Sexual and Gender Identity Disorders" for the American Psychiatric Association's most recent edition of the DSM (*Diagnostic and Statistical Manual of Mental Disorders*). The DSM is *the* resource consulted by mental health professionals all over the United States to diagnose their clients. So, this guy had literally written the book on transgender kids.

And he said that everything I was doing was wrong. Gender in young children was malleable, he said. Parents should take this into account and exert their influence and act before it was too late. He advocated what he called "limit setting" on cross-gender behavior in young children. He told parents to prohibit activities and interests that didn't match ones associated with the child's biological sex. So boys who wanted dolls and dresses should be redirected toward sports and trucks. Girls who said they were boys should be steered to dresses and dolls.

It made sense. It sounded reasonable. And I had tried a version of this myself, as had most of the parents I knew with kids like mine. Maybe we just didn't try hard enough. Or maybe we didn't do it right. This man claimed a success rate of nearly 90 percent. He said close to 90 percent of the kids in his clinic were "cured" of their cross-gendered affliction. Under his care, they had been spared a transgender life, which was this doctor's stated goal.

De-trans-ification
ray

I decided to learn more about this doctor and the research behind his theories. I borrowed his book from the library and tracked down some of the papers he had published in academic journals. His writings were full of case studies about the children he had worked with over the years. And these case studies included a great deal of detail about their mothers, especially ones like me with kids like mine, whom he referred to as "boys with gender identity disorder."

Apparently mothers like myself had serious problems.

A "substantial percentage" of us, the doctor wrote, were "emotionally or psychiatrically impaired." His book is packed with detailed accounts of our mental disorders: borderline personality, anxiety disorder, depression, impaired social adaptation, insecure attachment. It was his opinion that these impairments explained our inability to set "appropriate limits" on our children's inappropriate behaviors, including "cross-gender behavior in boys."

Was the doctor correct? *Was* I to blame? He had a fancy degree and ran a world-renowned clinic. He had published books and claimed to have science on his side. He also claimed he could cure our kids, rescuing them from a lifetime of medical interventions and outsider status. But I smelled a rat.

It seemed impossible for mothers like me to get it right. In one case study, the problem was identified as "maternal unavailability." In another, the doctor blamed "an inordinate amount of time" spent with the mother. *Which was it?* Was I too close to my child, or not close enough? The book didn't say. In other cases, the explanation for gender confusion in our "sons" was more straightforward: We hated men.

All this mother blaming felt tired and outdated. It also begged the question: Why did blame need to be assigned at all? What crime were we really being blamed for? The crime of having children who were different? Was it actually pathological to be a boy who loved dresses? Or to be a boy who was really a girl? Or was something else to blame? Were our kids sick or was something else sick?

I thought of Leelah Alcorn, and of the final words of her suicide note. "My death needs to mean something," she had written. "Fix society. Please."

---

## American Psychological Association

### FACT SHEET: Gender Diversity and Transgender Identity in Children[7]

The gender affirmative model is grounded in the evidence-based idea that attempting to change or contort a person's gender does harm. Psychological interventions should aim to help children understand that their gender identity and gender expression are not a problem. Providers should aim to non-judgmentally accept the child's gender presentation and help children build resilience and become more comfortable with themselves, without attempting to change or eliminate cross-gender behavior. Children who experience affirming and supportive responses to their gender identity are more likely to have improved mental health outcomes. Gender identity is resistant, if not impervious to environmental manipulation. Moreover, attempts to change a child's gender may have a negative impact on the child's well-being.

---

◈

MY PODCAST STARTED GAINING quite a few listeners and I started to get more emails. Some were hard to read, let alone respond to:

Gendermom,

I'm 14 years old and I know I'm a girl like your daughter. My parents say it's a phase. That I'll grow out of it. But I know they are wrong. I can't go on like this. If I can't be a girl, I don't want to live.

A friend said I should consult a lawyer before responding. Another said it could be a hoax, a malicious troll trying to lure me in and find out my real name in order to harass us. But I didn't think so. More emails came, very much like this one, from other young people. One boy was only eleven. They all wanted my advice. How could they convince their parents? They were all running out of hope. How could they endure the unimaginably long time until they reached 18 and could decide for themselves?

I did not want to write to other people's children. There was too much I could not know: whether their parents were kind or cruel, whether speaking up would be liberating or dangerous, whether hope was years away or right around the corner. Whether they were even transgender.

But I thought of Leelah, and I wrote them back and said all the things I did know to be true:

You are beautiful.

You deserve kindness and love.

I believe in you.

Whatever happens, you must not give up hope.

Please don't give up.

I WAS ALSO GETTING quite a few emails like this:

> I am sure you mean well, Gendermom, but I think you have
> taken this way too far. When I was a kid, I wanted to be a
> dog. That didn't make me one.

I couldn't argue with that. I didn't know any dogs who used to be children. But I also knew that this was different. The problem was proving it.

Whether I was up against skeptical relatives, psychologists with fancy titles and mommy issues, or random readers of my blog, at the end of the day, my best evidence was my seven-year-old herself—and the fact that she was happy in the completest possible sense: content, unworried, playful, loving, curious and excited about the possibilities of each new day. And so were the other young transgender children I had met, once they were heard and seen for who they said they were.

This was real, and it was right. Our children were not asking to be dogs. They were asking to be happy. But a thousand moms like me couldn't prove this. Our children's happiness needed to be quantified somehow, for it to have teeth. Better yet (as I was told by a friend who was a psychologist), it needed to be published in a peer-reviewed scientific journal.

I heard about a study underway at the local university that was recruiting young kids like mine—transgender or gender-nonconforming children, from age three to age twelve. I signed my daughter up, and soon we made our first visit to their lab, a dilapidated little building on the edge of the grand and sprawling campus of the University of Washington.

A young research assistant sat down for a chat with my daughter. "So, I have some games and questions about boys and girls," she said. "Do you want to play them with me?"

M. grinned shyly. "Yes."

"Great. So the first question is: *What is your physical body? A boy? A girl? Neither? Both?*"

"Probably girl," my child said.

"And what do you feel like on the inside?"

M. crossed her arms and frowned. This game wasn't turning out to be much fun. "When do we get to play?"

While they chatted, I filled out a long survey.

*Which cross-gender behaviors did you first notice?*

*Which cross-gender behaviors does your child exhibit now?*

*Please check the box if your child's preferences are typical of boys, girls, or neutral.*

The study, called the TransYouth Project, began in 2013. When we joined a year later, they had signed up about eighty families from around the US and Canada. They planned to track our children for the next twenty years. It would be the world's first long-term study of children like mine.

---

"What is the life of a kid who as a young child identifies as transgender, going to look like? And how will a parent's or an environment's decisions influence what that outcome will be? We hope to be able to have those answers for parents, that they can read and say, 'OK, here are kids who for 10 years have been living as their gender identity, and this is what they look like.' Maybe they have this particular likelihood of going to college, or being happy in relationships, things that we literally know nothing about.

This is really the first generation of kids who are having the option of living as their gender identity in everyday life. They are totally historic, they are paving the way, and we just know so little about what life will look like for them."[8]

—Dr. Kristina Olson, professor of psychology, Princeton
University, and founder of the TransYouth Project

---

I interviewed the lead researcher, Dr. Kristina Olson, for an episode of my podcast. What she told me gave me goose bumps, because her study was seeking answers to all of the questions that parents like me were asking—and it had already answered a big one. According to Dr. Olson, there is solid scientific evidence that my child saying she was a girl was (as I had suspected) *not* the same thing as her wanting to be a dog.

Dr. Olson explained that her team had used a technique called an "implicit association test" (IAT). Rather than asking children direct questions, this type of test solicits an automatic and unconscious response. During our visit to the lab, my daughter had played a "game" on the computer in which she was asked to look at the screen and then press two different keys on the keyboard "as fast as you can." One key should be pressed when she saw an image of a girl or a word that related to oneself (such as the words *I*, *me*, or *mine*). The other key should be pressed for "boy" images or words *unrelated* to oneself (words like *they* or *them*). Then, after a few minutes, the instructions were switched, and my daughter was told to press the same key for "boy" images and the words *I* and *me*. The other button was now for "girl" and "not me" words like *they* and *them*.

I was a little confused by this, but apparently that was the idea. By pressing the keys quickly, without pausing to think it through, the IAT reveals "implicit" information about how we view ourselves. As Dr. Olson explained, "People are much faster to associate two concepts if they're closely tied in their mind. So we can look at the relative speed of doing those two different associations."

In previous studies using this method, cisgender girls had been much quicker to associate "self words" (*I* or *me*) with images of girls, while cisgender boys were faster at associating these words with images of boys. Olson's study also tested cisgender kids as controls in her study, and then compared their scores with the transgender children. What they found was that transgender girls had test results indistinguishable from those of the cisgender girls.

"You can't tell by looking at someone's IAT score whether they are a transgender girl or a gender-typical girl." Olson told me that this suggests my child's proclamations of girlhood are *not* the same thing as another child expressing a wish to be a golden retriever. "This is something deeper about how they see their own gender identity." These findings were published in the journal *Psychological Science* in 2015.

The TransYouth Project is now following more than three hundred children. I feel incredibly lucky that we get to be a part of this historic study. I also feel a little jealous of the parents who, twenty years from now, will have answers to the questions I'm still asking.

---

In 2018, Dr. Kristina Olson became the first social scientist to be awarded the National Science Foundation's prestigious Alan T. Waterman Award.[9] The award includes a one-million-dollar research grant.

Later that same year, Dr. Olson was honored with a MacArthur Foundation Fellowship, commonly known as the "genius grant," in recognition of her contributions to "advancing the scientific understanding of gender."[10]

---

❖

OUR GIRLS WERE ALL dressed up and were hysterical with excitement. I had purchased our tickets months in advance, as soon as they went on sale. So did Alice, for her and Olivia, who was now fourteen. The sold-out event was packed. We made our way to the ballroom and grabbed four open seats a few rows from the front. M. stood up on her chair and looked around the crowded hall. "Is she here yet? I wanna see her!"

A woman waved at Alice and walked over to us. "So good to see you!" She spotted M., standing on her chair, trying to peer over the heads of the crowd. "What a beautiful green dress!"

"Yes, it is," M. said. "I wore it for Laverne. I think she will like it."

"I do, too. Do you want to meet her?"

It turned out that Alice's friend was one of the organizers of the event. She said she'd add our names to the list for the small private reception after Laverne's talk. While the girls started squealing, it occurred to me that they seemed to be the only children in the entire audience.

And then Laverne walked into the hall and everyone went nuts.

It was like a rock concert. M. was jumping up and down and clapping and screaming with Olivia. On the drive there, I had had to remind her who Laverne Cox was. "Remember that beautiful lady on the cover of the magazine?"

"I think so."

I don't think she did. I also don't think she understood much of what Ms. Cox said in her talk, though she clapped when the rest of us clapped, and laughed when we laughed. As I watched her, I hoped my seven-year-old was at least absorbing the one thing I wanted her to remember about this night: that the woman up on the stage, who was smart and beautiful and powerful and famous, was transgender.

*She's transgender like you, honey.*

---

"I stand before you an artist, an actress, a producer (an Emmy-winning producer), a sister, and a daughter, and I believe that it is important to name the various intersecting components of my multiple identities, because I am not just one thing."

—Laverne Cox, in a speech at the University of Washington, May 5, 2015

---

After the talk, we made our way to the private reception hall, where my daughter grabbed a cookie off the buffet and then staked out a spot near some doors at the far end of the room. There were multiple entrances to the room, but she seemed sure that was the one Laverne would enter through. She just stood there, with her back to everyone else in the room, staring at the doors, like a puppy waiting for its owner to come home. A few minutes later, Laverne burst into the room. My daughter had picked the right doors.

Laverne waved a big Hollywood wave to the room and flashed a big Hollywood smile. She was wearing a blue-and-green dress, in almost the same colors as the sundress my daughter was wearing. In heels, she was nearly twice as tall as my child, which is probably why she didn't at first seem to notice the little girl who was blocking her path. But my daughter held her ground between Laverne and the cheering crowd, and looked up at her, waiting to be seen.

My daughter meets Laverne Cox

And then Laverne looked down at her, and smiled, and said, "Well, *hello*. What's your name, honey?"

"I'm M.," she said.

"Hello, M."

"And I'm trans."

I could hear people all around me gasp and say, "Did you hear what that little girl just said?"

Laverne seemed to be at a loss. She put her hands on her hips and looked around the room. "Is anyone *with* her?"

I stepped forward. "I'm her mom." Then I got tongue-tied in the face of celebrity and forgot how to speak like a normal human. I have no idea what I said.

But M. knew what to do. She asked Laverne for a hug.

Laverne crouched down to the floor and wrapped her arms around my daughter, who closed her eyes and rested her head against the star's bosom. I heard Laverne say, "Remember, honey. Transgender is beautiful."

I wrote down the story of my daughter meeting Laverne Cox and posted it on my blog, along with photos of her with Laverne, making sure none of them showed M.'s face. A few days later, the blog post went viral. I heard from *People* magazine and *The Today Show*, asking for permission to share the photos on their websites. A photo of my daughter with Laverne even ended up on the home page for *Time* magazine. I gave interviews to a handful of reporters about the exciting meeting between my seven-year-old trans daughter and the world's most famous transgender woman.

M. even gave an interview.

**Reporter:** You're a very impressive young lady!

**M. (age seven):** Yeah! Umm . . .

**Reporter:** Do you sort of understand why people are so excited about your story?

**M.:** Maybe because my mama wrote about me on her blog and I guess I sound really fun, and nice, and exciting. I don't really know.

BUT THERE WAS A PART of the story that I left out when I talked with the reporters. It didn't make it on my blog, either. It's what happened right after my daughter met Laverne Cox, as we were driving home through the dark, rainy night, when I heard a question come from the back seat.

"Mama, what's a coma?"

Before I bought our tickets for the event, I had emailed the organizers to ask if it would be appropriate for a seven-year-old child. I was told yes, definitely. But there were parts of the talk that were definitely *not* appropriate for a young child. I had tried to distract her and cover her ears during those parts. But, of course, doing that just makes a kid listen more intently. She didn't miss a thing.

I explained that comas happen sometimes when you get hurt, and your body sleeps for a while, to help you get well.

She said, "Mama, remember that stuff Laverne Cox said about those transgender women getting attacked?"

"Yeah," I said. "I remember."

"That's horrible."

"Yes, that is horrible."

After a short pause, she said, "I wish I were *born* a girl, so it won't happen to me."

Sometimes you have to lie to your children. I told her that those bad things definitely wouldn't happen to her. She wanted to know *why* they wouldn't happen to her. How did I *know* that for sure? She was just seven years old. She was too young for this. She needed to feel safe and it was *my* job to make sure that she

did. So I told her that those bad things that happened to transgender women only happened in bad parts of a big city that is
really, really, *really* far away from where we lived.

She wanted to know *which* city. I wish I'd had the presence of
mind to invent a city, but instead I blurted out the name of a
big city that I'd never visited and was pretty sure we wouldn't be
visiting any time soon. I said, "Detroit."

"Mama, let's not ever go to Detroit."

I promised her we wouldn't.

The reality was that my child was probably not at great risk
for the type of violence Ms. Cox had spoken of during her talk.
Nearly all of the victims she mentioned were trans women of
color, who are far more likely to be attacked and killed simply for
being themselves. My daughter was a privileged white child living
in a progressive part of the country. She was also young—too
young to be a threat to the fragile egos of men who find themselves desiring a beautiful trans woman, and who react with their
fists, or worse. But that would change one day. Detroit wouldn't
always be so far away.

It wasn't until later that night that the full import of my child's
words sunk in. *I wish I were born a girl.* Upon learning that being
a transgender girl could mean that people might want to hurt
her, that being a transgender girl could lead to scary things
called comas, the only solution she could fathom was to be
another kind of girl. The kind of girl no one questions. But not
a boy. Not for a second, not even when she imagined her own
little life on the line.

**M. (age seven):** Do a story about Mrs. Squeak.

**Me:** Who's Mrs. Squeak?

**M.:** A mouse.

**Me:** So what kind of a story do you want?

**M.:** Something with no problems. With nothing going missing, no one being sad or left out. Just like, a happy life. I do not like stories with violence or wars.

**Me:** I don't either.

**M.:** Maybe there can be a little problem. Like something a little tiny bit sad, like a girl not getting to buy something at the store she really wants.

**Me:** A small problem.

**M.:** And the exact next day she just gets to buy it.

**Me:** So you want me to tell a happy story.

**M.:** Yeah.

❖

LAUREN WROTE TO WISH ME a Happy Arbor Day. She never missed a holiday. "Did you know that Arbor Day was started in Nebraska?"

Usually just hearing from Lauren made my day, but I was low, and I told her so. I had been watching the news coverage of a controversy brewing in another state. There was an ugly scene on TV of a school board meeting. People were jeering and booing as a woman stood at a podium and made the case for a new policy to support transgender students in the school district. They held signs that said NO BOYS IN THE GIRLS BATHROOM! The meeting wasn't happening in my community, but what if it did?

"The world feels *mean*, Lauren," I wrote. "Why are people going after kids like mine? How will I protect my sweet little child? And how do you watch news like this and still get through your day?"

"Just keep going," she wrote back. "No matter what others say and do, it is important to just keep going."

I promised her I would.

❖

THE PRIVATE SCHOOL had turned out to be an excellent choice. The school hosted the gender training I had requested. The teachers and staff had been kind and supportive. Little Sophie had never breathed a word. When I eventually spoke with Sophie's parents about it, they were wonderful, too. And I confided in a few other parents, including Rory's mommies, who all took it in stride and treated it as the big deal that it wasn't.

But this gift came with a high price tag. Every spare penny went toward paying the tuition. Even with Alice's help, I spent hours in the car most days, inching through traffic between home and school and my office. As we piled into the car every morning to drive across town, I'd watch the neighbors strolling up the sidewalk, *walking* to school. I wondered: Was it really necessary for us to flee across town to stay safe? What if we could make it work, right here, in our own community, going to school with our neighbors? I toyed with this risky and appealing thought. My local school district already had policies in place that allowed

my daughter to use the girls' bathroom and locker rooms, as
well as play on the girls' sports teams. And with Laverne Cox
and Caitlyn Jenner making headlines, people seemed to be less
and less shocked by the idea of a little transgender girl. Maybe,
now that my daughter was a little older, a little more self-aware,
a little more able to keep her own secrets, we could try out a big
public school.

But first we had to make her girlhood *official*. I had heard
too many stories of trans kids getting outed at school when a
substitute teacher unwittingly read out their legal name from
a class list. After that, everyone knew that Janie had once been
John, and there was no going back. I wasn't going to risk that.
If I enrolled her in a big public school, it had to be as a girl. A
girl named M.

It turned out to be remarkably easy to turn M. into a legal
girl. I filled out some forms. I paid a fee. The next thing I knew,
her dad and I were sitting in a wood-paneled courtroom, waiting
our turn to be acknowledged by the black-robed judge. I crossed
all of my fingers and toes. I knew there were hostile judges who
would refuse to change a minor's name if they realized it was
for a gender change. A friend of mine had been given an angry
lecture on God's plan from a judge who sent her home to pray.

Our judge called our names and we stood while he squinted,
frowning, over the top of his reading glasses, reviewing our
papers. He signed them and wished us luck, but he didn't smile.
Instead he sighed and said, "You're definitely in uncharted waters
with this."

"We know," we said, and thanked him.

JUST OVER A MONTH after we started the whole process, a piece of paper arrived in the mail with the state's official seal and my daughter's new legal name printed on it. It said M., followed by her new middle name, which I had chosen. It was the name that would have been her first name if we'd known from the beginning that she was really a girl. I showed my daughter this important piece of paper. "Look." I pointed at two words. "See what it says?"

"Sss . . . ssex," she read. "Fee-male. Female?" She squealed and threw her arms around my waist.

I felt a flush of guilt that I'd waited until now to do this, because I *had* waited, stalled, and delayed as long as possible on taking this final, official step. I'd known for at least two years that there was no going back to boyhood. But making it legal would mean that all traces of my son would be gone. He wouldn't even exist on paper anymore. I was the only one who found this sad. My daughter was doing a little dance around the living room, humming to herself.

"Did you notice how it has your new name on it?"

She paused her dance to come take another look. "Not *new* name," she corrected me. "*Real* name."

I called up the school district to ask about enrolling my child for second grade. "I think she's already in your system," I said. I had enrolled her two years previously, for kindergarten, before I decided to send her to the small private school. I told the person

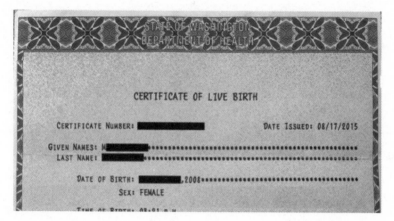

CERTIFICATE OF LIVE BIRTH

CERTIFICATE NUMBER: ████████████  DATE ISSUED: 08/17/2015

GIVEN NAMES: █████████•••••••••••••••••••••••••••••••••••••••••••••
LAST NAME: █████████•••••••••••••••••••••••••••••••••••••••••••••

DATE OF BIRTH: ██████████, 2008••••••••••••••••••••••••••••••••••••
SEX: FEMALE

My daughter's revised birth certificate

on the phone that my child had since changed her name and gender. "You'll need to send us the documents showing the change, and we'll update the record," I was told.

"But she never actually attended a school in the district," I said. So there were no records—no grades, no test scores, nothing—associated with her. Just a name and an ID number. Couldn't we just erase that old record and start fresh?

"You'll need to send us the documents showing the change and we'll update the record."

I wrote down where to send the court papers and the revised birth certificate. Then I hung up the phone and started considering. It would *probably* be fine. Surely the school district would be careful with our documents, and their records would be sealed, perhaps by law, from public view. But it still worried me, and it also irked me. Why did they need to know that I once thought my daughter was my son? Why must I send these precious papers—saturated with our story of confusion and loss, and also joy and redemption—for processing by a faceless bureaucracy?

Then I had a bold and daring thought for someone who had never even had a speeding ticket.

I called the school district again and asked, "Do you have students' social security numbers in your system?"

"No, we do not have social security numbers."

"Great, thanks for your help."

I then enrolled a brand-new student in the public school system. Her name was M. She was a girl.

I thought about what might go wrong: Someone might notice that there were two children with the same exact birthday, the same last name, the same home address, the same mother. Fraternal twins? But was anyone going to take the time to investigate this oddity, even if they noticed it? If I got caught, how serious was the infraction?

No one ever questioned me about the old record, about the boy living at my address who never showed up at school. But I thought of him sometimes. I thought about that abandoned ID number sitting there, for the boy who never grew up. The boy who had no grades, no test scores, no attendance records, no diploma. His life paused forever at age five.

# Make a plan.

My daughter was enrolled at the neighborhood elementary school, where she would start second grade in the fall. But the same unanswerable questions remained. These were all the same questions I had asked two years before, when she started kindergarten. Did I advise her to be open and tell everyone? Or did I encourage her to keep it to herself? If she did tell, would she later regret it? These same kids would be with her in middle school and then in high school. How could a seven-year-old possibly understand what all this would mean to her—and to her peers—when they were teenagers? How could I prepare her without scaring her?

I polled the other parents at the support group. Most of their kids seemed to be "stealth," telling no one or very few people at their schools. Some of their kids hadn't even told their closest friends, which I thought sounded unimaginably lonely and stressful, to always be holding something back, always fearing discovery. I combed through the emails I had received from readers of my blog. There were quite a few from teenagers. One had lost all her friends when the news got out at school. Another was threatened with rape by a boy who had been flirting with her before he knew she was trans.

"Secrets are toxic," a friend said to me.

"So is bullying," I countered. Her children were not transgender.

Lauren advised caution. "Once people know, they invariably treat you differently," she wrote. Lauren had followed the instructions the doctors at Stanford gave her in the 1970s: Do not reveal your status as a transsexual. Start over someplace new. Tell no one, blend in, become part of the woodwork. "I have been 'woodworked' for more than forty years," Lauren told me. "Of course, this isn't the right choice for everyone, but one thing is for sure: Once that genie is out of the bottle, you can't put it back in."

In the end, I told my daughter it was up to her. She could tell no one or everyone, or just some of the kids. But the last option was tricky, I said.

"Why is it tricky, Mama?"

"Because it can be hard for people to remember not to share things. Sometimes they forget that things are private." We used the word *private* a lot, and we avoided the word *secret*, with its undertones of shame and fear. Instead, it was just her private business, like which boy she had a crush on. And she could share it—or not—as she saw fit.

I reached out to the school counselor and a few weeks later, my ex and I sat down on turquoise child-size plastic chairs in her office. Once again, I spilled our story of how our daughter came to be our daughter, as breathless and nervous as the first time I told it. The school counselor was older, probably close to my mother's age. She must have seen it all, but she apparently hadn't seen anything quite like us.

She said they'd never had a transgender kid at the school before, but she smiled and said she was eager to learn. My daughter's second grade teacher sat next to her. Like the kindergarten teacher at the private school, she seemed nervous. And whenever I talked, she took notes.

Just like kindergarten, we all agreed that except for the school nurse, no one outside the room would be told that our daughter was transgender. My daughter had decided that she didn't want anyone else to know at her new school. She said she was afraid of being teased by the other kids if they found out.

No one was going to find out, if we didn't tell them. I explained to the counselor and teacher how our daughter was incredibly discreet, dressing in layers and always double-checking to make sure the bathroom stall door was firmly locked. The counselor said she thought we were in great shape and it seemed like our meeting was wrapping up. But I needed something else.

I said we needed a plan, just in case. What were we going to do if certain things happened? What scenarios could we strategize in advance? What if, in spite of all our precautions, a parent found out and got upset and complained? What if a rumor started and the kids started teasing her?

The counselor praised me for being so thoughtful about all this. She sat and waited for me to go on. The teacher lifted her pen, ready to take more notes. Weren't *they* supposed to tell me what to do when things went awry at school? Were these professional educators really stumped by a child like mine? I guess they were. I looked the teacher right in the eyes. "OK here's the deal," I said. "Here's what you do in 99.999 percent of the scenarios that could arise: If anyone asks, or has a problem, you just say, 'We don't talk about other people's private business. And certainly not about their private *parts*.'"

We all chuckled. It was so simple and so obvious, right? The veteran counselor gave me a warm nod. The teacher bit her lip and wrote something down. We thanked them and left.

> **Me:** You told her? When did you tell her?
>
> **M. (age seven):** I trusted her.
>
> **Me:** Did you explain about privacy?
>
> **M.:** Yes. I told her, "Please don't tell anyone."

❖

A FEW WEEKS BEFORE school started, I found out that my daughter had confided in a little girl in our neighborhood. Daisy lived just a block away. She and my daughter had spent the summer having marathon playdates and becoming best friends. Daisy would also be starting second grade at the neighborhood school.

Daisy's mom already knew. I had adopted a policy of always telling the parents before any playdates. It seemed safest to get it out of the way right up front. Daisy's mom was great about it. She and I had become good friends, too.

But Daisy was only seven years old. Was it realistic, or even fair, to ask such a young child to keep something like this to herself?

Walking to school on the first day of second grade

SECOND GRADE STARTED OUT really well. M. liked her teacher and was making lots of new friends. But then she started talking about her troubles with Daisy, who was jealous of M.'s new friends. A few weeks into the school year, M. came home and announced that she had told her favorite new friend, Lucy, that she was transgender. She said she might have also told her pal Cora, but she wasn't sure. "Don't worry, Mama. Lucy promised she wouldn't tell anyone."

I realized I had just sent my kid into the lion's den, alone and unarmed. What was I thinking? What if she told the wrong kid, who had the kind of parents who *wouldn't* be OK with a little girl with a penis in the bathroom? What would happen then? My child had no idea how badly this could go for her. She also didn't understand that you can't tell little kids to keep secrets from their parents these days. Especially about anything that could be interpreted as sexual, because that's what perverts and pedophiles do.

Of course, I knew that there was nothing sexual about my daughter's secret. She was seven years old and completely inno-cent about sex. She knew that private parts were kind of silly and embarrassing, but that was because adults made a big deal about keeping them covered up, and because they were used for going to the potty. She had no idea anyone might use them for something else. However, the only thing the other parents were likely to hear was this: Someone with a penis was using the girls' bathroom—and it was a secret their children had been told not to share.

I sat my daughter down and explained the new plan. I said that, of course, *she* got to decide whom she told that she was transgender. And I agreed that it was totally reasonable to ask her friends to keep this information to themselves. "But if you do want to tell another friend at school, then please tell me first." I told her that I would talk to the parents of her friend, and then, after that, if I said it was OK, she could tell the friend. "Does that make sense, sweetheart?"

She was fidgeting with a pile of LEGOs and didn't seem to be listening. I asked her to put them down and give me her attention. "But this is boring!" She looked angry and confused. No wonder she was confused. I was making this far too complicated, and I always seemed to be contradicting myself. I was always telling her that there was nothing wrong or weird about being transgender. But if that were true, why did we have to be so cautious about telling other people? Why did the simple fact of sharing her identity with a friend have to set in motion an elaborate plan involving adults she had never met?

She muttered something into her pile of LEGOs.

"What did you say?"

"I didn't think that they needed to know anything about it."

"The other parents?"

"Yeah."

The kid had a point. *Did* these other parents really need to know? Did they have a right to know?

Then again, maybe all this focus on "privacy" was a mistake. Maybe secrets really *were* toxic. Maybe it *would* be better to just tell everyone, to rip off the Band-Aid and put it out there. We'd know once and for all who our friends were. I told my daughter we could do that if she wanted. "Sometimes it's just too much work to keep something really private." I said it might be easier if everyone knew, so she wouldn't have to worry about people finding out. "Does that make sense, sweetheart?"

She smashed a fist into her LEGOs. "No sense at all."

A few days later, my daughter told me that if anyone besides Lucy found out that she was transgender, she was going to have to switch schools. She said she was scared that if the other kids found out she was transgender, something really bad would happen.

"What bad thing would happen?" I asked.

"I'm afraid they will kill me."

Dear gendermom,

As a Black mother to two Black children, I understand your dilemma. My son is only eight, but we have already taught him not to raise his voice or react when he's upset, not to call attention to himself.

It crushes my soul to say it, but our kids will not get to have a childhood. Not in the same way as other kids. They don't get to just be free, because the stakes are higher for them.

❖

ALICE SUGGESTED THAT I ASK the teacher if she'd consider presenting a lesson on gender in the classroom. It seemed like a perfect solution: If the kids in her class were told what it meant to be transgender, and that there was nothing wrong with it, and my daughter could *witness* this, then she wouldn't have to be afraid of them finding out. And the ones who already knew would know that being transgender was OK.

M.'s teacher agreed, and so did the school counselor. There was even a woman in the school district headquarters who advocated for LGBT students in the district, and she offered to come give the lesson herself. After the classroom gender lesson was scheduled, I began wondering what the LGBT advocate would actually say to the kids. I figured the lesson would deal with gender stereotypes and maybe gay issues, but would she go all in? Would she say the word *transgender*? Could you *do* that in public school?

What I wanted was for my child to hear the thing that we called her—*transgender*—said out loud, explained, and embraced as normal, by an adult in charge, to the twenty-seven other little kids in her second-grade class. If the LGBT advocate didn't do *that*, what was the point?

I emailed the woman and asked her, straight up, if she would be doing this. I told her how afraid my daughter was. I told her that I believed hearing just a few choice words could change everything for her. Maybe it was too much to hope for. Maybe it was too much to ask for an official representative of a large public school district to tell a group of second graders that it's just fine to switch genders. I don't live in a red state, but still. I didn't hear back for a week and a half.

I'll always wonder what happened in that week and a half, in the world of the woman who got my email asking her to stick her neck out for my daughter. Was she just busy? Or was she spending all that time trying to figure out whether or not she could say yes to me? I imagined all sorts of strategizing and hand-wringing going on, over the politics and potential fallout, debating with her colleagues and her friends and her partner over the dinner table. Finally, after ten days, I heard from her.

She said she would discuss gender roles and stereotypes, and the importance of respecting differences. She would also explain to the children what *transgender* was. She planned to read the new children's book *I Am Jazz* to the class. After appearing on *20/20* with Barbara Walters, Jazz Jennings had become an outspoken advocate for trans kids, with a popular YouTube channel and her own reality show on TV. We already owned a copy of Jazz's book. It told a story very much like ours. My daughter adored it.

> "My best friends are Samantha and Casey. We always
> have fun together. We like high heels and princess gowns, or
> cartwheels and trampolines.
> But I'm not exactly like Samantha and Casey.
> I have a girl brain but a boy body.
> This is called transgender.
> I was born this way!"
> —*I Am Jazz*, by Jessica Herthel and Jazz Jennings

The morning of the classroom gender lesson, I received an email from the teacher. She wrote that they had just finished the lesson and it had gone well. The kids had really liked the book about Jazz. After the woman from the district left, my daughter walked up to the teacher and whispered in her ear that she wanted to tell the whole class that she was transgender.

The teacher asked her if she was sure about this, and my daughter said, "I'll think about it." I was at work. I thought about hopping in my car and driving to school and grabbing her out of the classroom, before something happened that we couldn't undo.

I could see the whole scene in my mind: My daughter walking up to the teacher, feeling proud and special, because she was like the cool transgender girl in the story that everyone liked so much. It made me so happy to think of it that way. But I also felt incredibly sad, because her teacher responded exactly how I would have responded: Are you *sure?* Are you sure you should be honest about who you are?

An hour later, another email from the teacher landed in my inbox. My daughter had come up with another plan. She said she wanted to tell her three best friends in the class: Lucy and Cora, who probably already knew, and one other little girl. The teacher offered to arrange for the girls to eat lunch in the classroom instead of the cafeteria, so they'd have privacy when my daughter told them, and so she could oversee it and help out if the kids had questions. She suggested I talk this over with my daughter that night and email her back to let her know what we wanted her to do.

That night I told M. that I'd heard from her teacher about her plan to tell her friends. I said it sounded like a great plan, but that I wanted to talk with the girls' parents first. I hated having to say that. But she agreed to wait until I had talked to the parents of her three little friends.

I spent the following week tracking down the mothers of the three girls, none of whom I had ever met. I sent each of them a cryptic email, in which I said that I wanted to meet to talk with them about our daughters. Over coffee, perhaps? I didn't tell them what I wanted to talk about, but I reassured them that it wasn't anything bad. This invitation must have been simultaneously intriguing and unsettling, because they all made time to meet me right away.

I met them, one by one, face-to-face, over lattes, at a nearby Starbucks. I didn't beat around the bush. "I bet you're wondering what the heck this is about!" I said, as soon as we sat down, laughing to keep it light. Then I launched into the phrases I'd become so accustomed to reciting over the past three years: *She's just always been like this. . . . She's never wavered since she first told me at age three. . . . She just wants to be seen as a regular girl.* One by one, they listened, eyes widening, forgetting to drink their lattes, saying nothing.

I rushed on, filling the awkward silence. I explained how unexpected and confusing this had all been, this transgender thing, so they'd understand that I was surprised just like them. I told them how desperately sad it made M. to be seen as a boy, so they'd understand how important this was. I told them how private my daughter was about it, so that they would understand why I was asking them not to tell any other parents. And so they'd know that she wasn't flashing a penis around the bathroom, and that she was not any kind of threat to their little girls.

I told them how scared she was of being teased, and of being excluded or bullied. I could hear myself getting breathless again, worried I might leave out some critical detail; worried I would fail to make them see that my daughter's transgender girlhood was not only real, but entirely innocent, and also utterly vulnerable. "Not everyone accepts us," I said, hoping they'd see what I was trying to say with my eyes: *You now have the power to help us or hurt us. Please be kind.*

I closed with a compliment, to sweeten my case. "She only wants to tell her *special* friends, the ones she really trusts, and she picked *your* daughter." The first mom teared up and fished in her purse for a tissue. She said I was "courageous." Then she changed the subject. Was my daughter going to join the soccer team?

The second mom was very, very quiet. I told her that I was happy to answer any questions she had. Anytime, anything, just ask. "I know it's a new thing for a lot of us," I said. She didn't have any questions, she said. Her smile was tight and thin. Was that how she always smiled? She said she really had to leave to pick up her son.

I was most nervous about the third and final mom. Daisy's mom had tipped me off that this mom attended a very conservative church. It was an urban megachurch not far from my house. Its charismatic young pastor had been in the local news for making homophobic comments in his sermons and advising his female parishioners to assume a subservient role in their marriages. I doubted he'd be telling his flock that they should be fine with a transgender second grader. I considered telling my daughter that maybe she *shouldn't* tell the daughter of mommy number three, but I just didn't have the stomach for that. I decided to risk it.

For the third time, I delivered my breathless spiel. Mommy number three took a long, slow sip of her latte, then set it down and studied her paper cup. I held my breath. She looked me in the eyes and said, "We're all made in the image of God."

The next day, the teacher let my daughter and her three friends eat lunch in the classroom. M. told the girls she was transgender, like Jazz in the book. And that was it, the teacher said. They finished their lunches and ran off to recess. That night I emailed the three moms to tell them how it had gone and to thank them. Mommy number one wrote back, but there was no reply at all from the other two moms. I wondered if we'd just made a really big mistake.

# *Fight back.*

Up until this point, transgender kids had been virtually invisible. I had struggled to convince people that someone like my child even existed. Now the world was finally paying attention, finally acknowledging people like my daughter, and it seemed to think that they were dangerous. All of a sudden, everyone on the news was talking about where transgender people should—and shouldn't—pee.

Around the country, legislators were debating so-called bathroom bills targeting transgender people and designed to mandate who was allowed to use which bathroom. Some of the proposed laws required you to use the bathroom matching the gender on your birth certificate. Some required that you use the one that matched the "parts" in your pants, or that aligned with your DNA. It wasn't at all clear how these laws might be enforced, but their proponents claimed they were needed to protect women and girls from being attacked in the ladies' room by men posing as women. Opponents of the bathroom bills argued that this was baseless fearmongering, and that the people most likely to be assaulted in restrooms were transgender people themselves.

I could see why the arguments for the other side seemed so compelling. If a bunch of ill-intentioned men were indeed sneaking into women's locker rooms under the cover of laws intended to protect transgender rights, that would be a scary scenario. I didn't want those men in the bathroom with me either, and certainly not with my precious little girl. But it all turned out to be a red herring; there just wasn't any evidence that men posing as transgender women were infiltrating changing rooms and bathrooms. When I found out that the national organizations backing these laws were the same right-wing groups that had fought against legalizing same-sex marriage, I realized this fight probably had nothing at all to do with ensuring the safety of women while we pee.

I took some comfort from the fact that these debates were taking place elsewhere—far away, in more conservative states like Texas and South Dakota. I felt safe and snug in my blue-state home on the West Coast, where there had been a law on the books for ten years protecting the rights of transgender people to use the bathroom matching their gender identity.

Everything changed a few weeks after Christmas, in the damp, gray heart of a Seattle winter, when a bathroom bill suddenly stormed into town. And I did not feel so safe anymore.

> SPOKANE, Wash.—The Washington State Senate is taking up a bill aimed at overturning the controversial law that allows transgendered people to use the restrooms or even locker rooms of the gender they identify with.
>
> Opponents of the law argue that it puts women in danger.
>
> The law in question has actually been around for a decade, but the rule, which was enacted in December, clarifies some antidiscrimination laws that have been in place since 2006. It was that clarification that brought into focus concerns about sex offenders potentially abusing the laws to find victims.
>
> —KXLY news, January 29, 2016[11]

I TOOK A DAY OFF work to drive to the state capitol in Olympia and attend a public hearing on the bill. All the parents in our support group were fired up. We would pack the senate hearing with our outrage. We would show those conservative senators that they'd picked the wrong state to pick on trans people.

The night before the hearing, my daughter overheard me talking about it on the phone with my mom and asked me about it. I told her that I was going to a gathering to support transgender rights. I tried to spin it so it wouldn't sound scary—more like a party or a parade than a fight. She had just turned eight, but she was still too young for this.

She said it sounded fun. "Can I come?"

"Maybe next time."

At the capitol, I shuffled through a packed hallway, my ears pounding from the voices of hundreds of fellow citizens echoing off the marble walls. I tried to find my friends. As I wedged my way slowly through the crowd, I brushed sleeves over and over again with rain-spattered coats, nearly all of them adorned with the same red-white-and-blue sticker. The sticker said KEEP LOCKER ROOMS SAFE.

This was one of the confusingly compelling slogans adopted by people supporting the bathroom bill. Who *didn't* want safe locker rooms and bathrooms? If only these safety-minded citizens could see my daughter, age seven, every time she used a public restroom, double- and triple-checking to make sure the stall door was locked tight. And then doing her business as fast as she could, because, as she told me, she was worried someone might peek underneath the stall and spy on her and see something and judge her.

We had been advised not to engage the other side, but I couldn't help myself. I wanted someone to see just who it was they thought they were so scared of. As we stood in the stuffy hall waiting for the hearing room doors to open, I showed a woman next to me a picture of my daughter. The woman was a little older than I was. I assumed she had children, perhaps grandchildren, of her own. And she smiled at the photo in the knowing way a fellow mother often does. The woman had a red-white-and blue sticker on the front of her sweater. "She's transgender," I said, pointing to my daughter's picture. She stopped smiling and waved the photo away.

I finally found my friends in the crowd, and we hugged like years had passed, and then stood together in silence in our small, stickerless circle. I left them briefly to find the bathroom, and before I got back, the hearing room opened and filled up completely. I was turned away at the door and joined a crowd heading to the overflow area in the senate gallery, where a live video showed us what was going on in the hearing room.

The gallery filled up fast, too, until it was standing-room only. Some friendly women around my mother's age smiled and made space for me to squeeze in next to them on a wooden bench. I felt like I was at my childhood church, sitting in a polished wooden pew with ladies who looked familiar and nice, the kind of ladies who would have let me take extra cookies at coffee hour. They noticed I didn't have a safe-locker-rooms sticker and offered to help me find one.

On the video, a young male senator introduced the bathroom bill, which he had sponsored. He said it was designed to keep men out of women's locker rooms. He said parents didn't want their little girls in the bathroom with boys at school. The ladies next to me nodded. I squirmed in my seat. *My daughter is not a boy*, I whispered to myself. *You're wrong. You're all making a terrible, dangerous mistake.*

Then members of the public came to the microphone and spoke in support of the bill. They warned that pedophiles and human traffickers would fill the state's public restrooms and locker rooms. They said that if we didn't pass this bill, we were sacrificing the safety of women and children in order to pander to a "vocal minority."

I was holding my daughter's photo in my lap. Her hair was now down to her shoulders. She was posing like a Hollywood starlet, in her new red dress and the pink patent leather slippers her grandmother had given her for Christmas. How could anyone expect this person to use the men's room?

I shivered when the next speaker came to the microphone and suggested that we consider finding "a place that's separate" for transgender people to pee. I recalled what I'd heard a transgender woman say in the hallway before the hearing: "They don't just want us gone from the bathrooms. They want us gone, period."

One of the dads from our support group made a passionate case for our side. "How do I explain to my sweet little girl," he asked the senators, "when I tuck her in at night, that she can't use the girls' bathroom, because people who make our laws think that there's something wrong with her?"

Our support group facilitator was there, too, calm and wise as always. "The issue is neither a political issue nor a faith issue," he said. "It is simply one of everyone needing more information. Education and preparation are crucial."

My friends told me later that it was eerily quiet in the actual hearing room. In the senate gallery, however, where there were no senators to keep order, it was a different story. As each person spoke, cheers echoed through the senate chamber. Our side's cheers were pretty feeble compared to theirs, but I did my best, hooting and clapping for my friends when they spoke against the bill. The ladies who had made room for me in the pew looked surprised, and then they stopped making eye contact.

I knew that it was likely that these ladies, and probably the majority of the people there in support of the bathroom bill, believed that they had never met a transgender person, let alone a transgender child. I knew that many of them probably believed the claims that allowing transgender people bathroom access would fill the women's rooms with perverts and pedophiles. But I still felt like their cheers were bricks, thrown at me and my daughter.

I wondered if, under the right circumstances, in a place without marble hallways and senators keeping order, some of these people would throw actual bricks at us. The senate committee voted along party lines—four Republicans in favor, three Democrats opposed—to send the bill to the full senate for a vote.

❖

THE FACT OF A bathroom bill in my own backyard worked its way under my skin, making me wonder: Who were the people in my community who supported it? I worried anew about my neighbors, my coworkers, the other parents at school.

The text from Cora's mom said, "Sorry, we are busy this weekend." I suggested to M. that we try a different friend for a playdate.

My daughter stomped her foot. "But she was busy last time, too!"

"I know, it's a bummer. Cora's family seems to be really busy."

I texted back to Cora's mom: "Maybe next weekend?"

Cora's mom did not reply to this text. Or to the next three I sent after my daughter kept on begging me to secure a playdate with the elusive Cora. "She's my best friend at school," she said. "I really love her." I told her I'd keep trying, although there didn't seem to be much point. Maybe Cora's mom was just too busy to respond. Or maybe Cora didn't want to have a playdate with my daughter.

I didn't really believe that either of these things were true.

A few weeks later, the full Washington State senate voted on the "bathroom bill." Our side won by just one vote. That spring the state legislature in North Carolina passed its infamous bathroom bill, sparking even more national headlines and debates about where my daughter should do her business.

> *The New York Times*
> NORTH CAROLINA BANS LOCAL ANTI-DISCRIMINATION POLICIES
> By Dave Phillips
> March 23, 2016
>
> North Carolina legislators, in a whirlwind special session on Wednesday, passed a wide-ranging bill barring transgender people from bathrooms and locker rooms that do not match the gender on their birth certificates.
>     Republicans unanimously supported the bill, while in the Senate, Democrats walked out in protest. "This is a direct affront to equality, civil rights and local autonomy," the Senate Democratic leader, Dan Blue, said in a statement.
>     North Carolina's governor, Pat McCrory, a Republican, signed the bill late Wednesday night.[12]

There was good news, too. The University of Washington study that was tracking my daughter and other transgender kids published its first set of findings. The researchers had found that young transgender children like mine, who were allowed to live in their preferred gender, appeared to be psychologically healthy, with scores on mental health measures essentially indistinguishable from their non-transgender peers. These findings contrasted sharply with multiple studies of kids who had not been allowed to socially transition. Those kids exhibited sky-high rates of depression and anxiety, triple that of healthy kids like mine. According to science, I *was* doing the right thing. I also learned that the Canadian psychologist—the one who had argued for decades that I was doing the wrong thing—had been fired, and his clinic shut down pending an investigation of its practices.

---

Previous work with children with gender identity disorder (GID; now termed gender dysphoria) has found remarkably high rates of anxiety and depression in these children. Here we examine, for the first time, mental health in a sample of socially transitioned transgender children. . . .

**RESULTS:** Transgender children showed no elevations in depression and slightly elevated anxiety relative to population averages. They did not differ from the control groups on depression symptoms and had only marginally higher anxiety symptoms.

**CONCLUSIONS:** Socially transitioned transgender children who are supported in their gender identity have developmentally normative levels of depression and only minimal elevations in anxiety, suggesting that psychopathology is not inevitable within this group. Especially striking is the comparison with reports of children with GID; socially transitioned transgender children have notably lower rates of internalizing psychopathology than previously reported among children with GID living as their natal sex.[13]

—Kristina R. Olson, PhD, et al., "Mental Health of Transgender Children Who Are Supported in Their Identities," *Pediatrics*, March 2016

---

It even looked like we had the president with us. It was in the spring of 2016, and I was with Alice when we heard the news. We huddled together on her living room couch, hunched over my phone, crying and laughing with joyous surprise, watching and rewatching the video of Attorney General Loretta Lynch, as she announced at a press conference that the Obama's administration was going to fight the bathroom bill in North Carolina. She said it violated our nation's laws and its values and compared it to the fear-fueled discrimination that led to Jim Crow laws and "separate but equal" schools for black children. Then Lynch, herself an African American woman who was born and raised in the state of North Carolina, said she wanted to speak directly to our community:

> Let me also speak directly to the transgender community itself. Some of you have lived freely for decades. Others of you are still wondering how you can possibly live the lives you were born to lead. But no matter how isolated or scared you may feel today, the Department of Justice and the entire Obama Administration wants you to know that we see you; we stand with you; and we will do everything we can to protect you going forward." (May 9, 2016)

Alice sniffed and wiped her eyes and said, "Hallelujah!" She opened a bottle of wine, and we toasted Loretta Lynch, the president, and our beautiful daughters, our daughters whom they finally saw, whom they had pledged to protect.

A few days later, Obama's justice department joined the education department to make another announcement. Henceforth, Title IX, the 1972 law prohibiting sex discrimination in public

education, would be interpreted as applying equally to transgender students. Practically, this meant that the highest law in
the land now said that my daughter had the right to be a girl at
school, when she peed and when she played sports and when she
changed for gym class.

But we were not out of the woods yet. After the bathroom bill
failed in the Washington State Senate, a private group immediately launched an initiative campaign to put a bathroom bill
on the ballot in the fall. If they got enough signatures, then my
daughter's rights would soon be up for public vote.

The initiative differed from the senate's failed bathroom bill.
Rather than just remove protections for transgender people, this
law specifically targeted school children. Initiative 1515 would
make it illegal for my daughter to use the girl's bathroom at
school. It also put a price on her head. If it passed, any parent
who believed their child had been in the girls' restroom with my
daughter could sue the school for 2,500 dollars, plus monetary
damages for the, "psychological, emotional, and physical harm
suffered" by their child, from having been in a bathroom with a
child like mine.

**Washington State Initiative Measure No. 1515,
filed March 24, 2016**

PART III

PUBLIC SCHOOLS MUST MAINTAIN SEX SPECIFIC
RESTROOM, TOILET, SHOWER, LOCKER ROOM, SAUNA, AND
CHANGING AREA FACILITIES

Sec. 3. (4)(e)

Any student who prevails in an action brought under this subsection (4) may recover from the defendant public school two thousand five hundred dollars for each instance in which they encountered a person of the opposite sex while accessing a public school student restroom, locker room, or shower room designated for use by the aggrieved students' sex. The student may also recover monetary damages from the defendant public school for all psychological, emotional, and physical harm suffered.[14]

I took another day off work to go to a rally against the bathroom bill initiative. This time I brought along some reinforcements, picking up my parents and my sister, Aunt M., on my way there. I didn't bring my daughter, but I did bring a poster she had made, a self-portrait that she labeled "Proud trans girl."

"Will the bad guys be there?" my mom asked.

"I don't know."

I was nervous we might encounter some ugly counterprotests and find ourselves face-to-face with the same people who had filled the marble halls at the state capitol. When we drove into the parking lot of the church hosting the rally, we saw burly security guys at the door. Inside, a TV news crew was setting up. We were handed bright red signs that said WASHINGTON WON'T DISCRIMINATE.

Then we sat in long wooden pews and listened to speeches, cheering and waving our red signs for the TV cameras. The pews were just like the wooden benches at the senate gallery. But this time, I sat between my dad and my sister, with my mom squeezed in next to her. This time, instead of no one around me supporting my daughter, everyone was. If anyone in the crowd supported the bathroom bill, they kept quiet.

The initiative backers claimed they had plenty of votes to pass it, were it to land on the ballot. The scary news making its way through the support group grapevine was that they were right. Both sides were saying it was expected to pass if it was put to a public vote.

I forced myself to imagine the worst, and to plan for it. One thing I could not imagine doing was sending my child to school with a bounty on her head. It was out of the question. I spoke with Alice and some other moms about the possibility of starting some sort of homeschool group of our own. If our kids couldn't safely attend public schools, maybe my daughter would finally realize her dream of attending an all-transgender school.

I wondered if leaving private school had been a mistake. It was now late in the spring, long past all the application deadlines for attending a private school in the fall. I wondered if one of them might make an exception for us. If the initiative passed, and it was suddenly open season on trans kids, would they offer refuge to a seven-year-old asylum seeker?

I called up my friend Tiffany from the support group. Her transgender son Skyler is the same age as my daughter. She listened with interest to my idea for starting an all-transgender school. Tiffany told me that after Skyler was hassled for using the boys' bathroom in first grade, he stopped using the bathroom at school completely.

> **Me:** What do you think, Dad? Are we gonna win?
>
> **M.'s Grandpa:** We're going to win because it's the right thing to do. This, too, will pass. This nightmare of hate, fostered by ignorance, fostered by those who don't understand or appreciate how joyful it is to be a loving human being.

"He . . . held it?"

"Yes. He just held it until it was harming him, quite frankly. It was *not* healthy."

I told her about the conversation I'd had with M. the night before. We were packing her clothes for a short vacation to visit friends in California when she announced that she could only wear "skorts and nothing else," and then broke down sobbing. "It's so hard getting dressed. I can't wear anything! I have to be so careful!"

I asked what she was worried about. "Are you afraid of getting teased if someone finds out?"

She shook her head. "No one will tease me. I just don't want people talking about me. Even if they are being nice."

How was I supposed to tell her that she might soon be the only girl in school barred from using the girls' bathroom? How was I going to explain that the people promoting the initiative had no intention of being nice to people like her?

She said she wished she hadn't told her friends at school. "I wish I could just wash their memories."

Tiffany groaned. "Oh, my darling."

"My kid is way too young to hear all this," I said. "She is *not* up for this."

"I know. These kids are having to grow up way too fast."

❖

A LITTLE GIRL WALKED UP to my daughter on the playground at recess and said, "I know your secret." Four little words that in almost any other context of young childhood would mean something like: *I know which boy you like. I know you stole Suzie's favorite pen. I know you're the one who forgot to lock Fuzzy's cage and now the class has no pet hamster.*

I. Know. Your. Secret.

Her name was Ella. Another little girl I had never heard of. "Do you think she was talking about the transgender thing?" I said, clinging to the faintest of hopes that this could be about Fuzzy.

My daughter rolled her eyes at my naivete. "What else would she be talking about?"

I knew it had always been a bold gamble, telling such young children and then asking them to keep it to themselves. Maybe it wasn't fair or realistic, to ask that of a second grader in the first place. Maybe it was ridiculous to think a secret this interesting could be trusted with anyone.

I texted my daughter's trans big sister and told her what had happened. "It's awful, but it's our reality," Anna texted back. "People always talk. I've been outed by a colleague at every single job I've ever had."

It must have been Cora, whose mother had ghosted us. Or maybe Lucy. I remembered her parents had turned down the invitation to my daughter's birthday party. Were they *really* busy that Saturday? I found myself desperate to know what had happened, to track the unkept secret back to its source so we could plug the hole, secure the breach.

Was Ella the only child who had been told? Could I stop this before it spread even further? Or was it already too late? Was it already time to pack up and relocate to a new school and start over? Or come clean and tell everyone?

"It was Daisy," my daughter said. "Daisy told her."

Anna sent another text: "Is she OK?"

"I think so. But I'm not," I replied.

It turned out that Ella was just one of three more little girls who were now in the know. Once again, I tracked down the names of three mothers I had never met. This time, I didn't bother with scheduling coffee dates. I asked the school to have them call me as soon as possible. Three more times, I rushed breathlessly through our story. And then, three more times, I made my desperate request: *Could you please ask your child not to tell?*

One mother was friendly; she said her best friend was gay. One was noncommittal; she needed to speak to her husband first. One was put out; she was *not* ready to talk with her daughter about this kind of thing yet, not when she was so young. It didn't seem "age-appropriate," she said. "But I guess I have no choice now."

"I'm sorry," I said, unsure which sin I was apologizing for.

Daisy's mom was horrified. Daisy was horrified and sorry. It had been a slip of the tongue, she said. She never meant to tell. It just came out. My daughter understood. She said she had spilled a secret once herself. She said she still loved her friend but wouldn't be telling her any more of her secrets. I wondered what others she could possibly have, and whether these might be better ones to start with next time.

# *Let go.*

went alone to the support group. It had been a long time since I was the one doing most of the crying. "My child's fate is now in the hands of a bunch of eight-year-old girls whose parents think I'm either crazy or some sort of sexual pervert."

I was given sympathetic smiles and the tissue box and stories that didn't make me feel any better. A nonbinary kid was being bullied in the school bathroom and told their parents they wanted to die. A transgender girl was quarantined to a section of the school playground after another parent hired an attorney and got a restraining order against her. She was nine years old.

Her parents planned to switch schools as soon as they could and go underground.

"I'm just so tired of putting out fires," I complained. The mother of Jazz Jennings had used those words in her interview with Barbara Walters about her transgender daughter. "I put out the fires before they burn her," she had said to Barbara. That's exactly what it felt like to me. But there always seemed to be another fire starting somewhere, and as I stamped it out, I was scanning the horizon for smoke.

"You can't put out *all* the fires, mama," the facilitator said.

"Watch me try," I growled at him.

"Don't forget that your kids are resilient," he said. "They are amazing people. They are the most courageous, resilient people you are likely to meet, of any age, anywhere." As usual, this man was right. It was true. All children are resilient marvels, and we all face trials, but our kids had done battle with mighty foes earlier than most.

How many of us would have the nerve to take on the world, as our children had done? How many of us would risk everything, including perhaps our own parents' love, in order to craft from scratch an outside life that matched our insides? How many would defy a system that society had declared immutable and inviolable, to trust instead some inner knowing, some essential drumbeat of self? And how many of us would summon the courage and clarity to give voice to that drumbeat and show the rest of us ways of being in the world that most of us had never seen or even imagined?

I thought of my child at four years old. How she had worked on me, day after day, week after week, with each small, sparkly request, each extravagantly feminine self-portrait, each stone laid reverently in her fairy garden. I thought of her standing on the stage at age four, head thrown back, singing a song she alone could hear, waiting for the rest of us to finally listen, to finally recognize the vital drumbeat of her girlhood: *See me, see me, see me.*

I thought about what the school counselor told me when she called to talk about Ella and my daughter's secret. "Your daughter is a wonder," she said. She told me my child had neither yelled at Ella nor panicked or cried, although no one would have blamed her if she had. Instead, she walked calmly up to the playground teacher and said that she needed to speak to the principal right away. I was surprised to hear this. She didn't really know the principal at all, but I suppose she figured it was best to go straight to the top. The counselor said my daughter walked into the principal's office that afternoon and told her that other kids were sharing her private things and this was wrong and she needed help to stop them.

By the time I heard about it, my daughter was already putting out the fire. Or maybe there was no fire, just another day like most days, where things are sometimes hard, and if you're transgender, or your child is, maybe they're extra hard, but you believe in yourself, you listen to your soul's quiet drumbeat, and you deal with them. Maybe this is all we really needed to know.

Dear Marlo,

I turn 64 years old next Sunday. I will cherish the day as
I cherish every day because, as you know from your own
experience with M., each day is a gift. I will always consider
myself saved from a life of unknown misery and sadness.

   You and I both know that M. will have some troubling
times ahead. I know she is quite young, but someday she
will have a better understanding of her unique place in this
rickety old world. She will understand that who she is and
what she stands for is very difficult for many people to grasp.
This is where she has to be brave and strong and keep her
eye on her goal. Please tell her that I know that she has a
wonderfully happy and loving future ahead. That I know
what she's going through and can assure her it is indeed all
worth it. Yes, it is all worth it.

Life is so grand!

My best to you both always,
Lauren

❖

THE SPRING RAINS had made a mess of M.'s fairy garden, which
was now home to half a dozen plastic fairies, a mouse with a wiz-
ard hat, and a Pegasus. The fairies' wings were splattered with
mud. The mouse lay facedown in the weeds. I suggested we take
them all inside for a quick bath in the kitchen sink.

"Not now," she said, looking sternly down at the dirty fairies like they were a disappointment to her. Instead we strolled up the block, hand in hand, admiring the neighbors' flowers. "Ella said I'm really a boy," she said to a lilac bush heavy with blossoms.

"Oh, sweetie, I'm so sorry."

We walked on in silence as I searched in vain for the right words to account for life's latest unfairness. None came, but I would fix this. Was it Ella's mom who had been so angry on the phone? Should I call her again? Should I call the teacher? The principal? I looked up and scanned the cloudy sky for the crack to be mended, and for the series of steps I must now take to repair our world.

I felt my daughter's hand squeeze mine. "Mama," she said. When I didn't respond, she shook my arm, shook me back to earth. "It's OK," she said. "I just told her."

"Told her what?"

"That I'm a girl. And that only I get to decide that I'm a girl. And that my mama said so."

EPILOGUE

Nearly five years have passed since that spring stroll with my daughter. A great deal has changed since then.

I met a wonderful man and got remarried (my daughter was the flower girl at our wedding). We moved to a different part of town, where she started fifth grade at a new school. She soon had a collection of new friends (nearly all girls). As before, she chose to tell her closest friends that she was transgender, and (so far) they have all been kind and loyal, as have their parents. This fall, she will start eighth grade.

One thing that hasn't changed is her unshakable assertion that she is indeed a girl. If you are wondering whether I have ever

> **Me:** What's your favorite thing about being transgender?
>
> **M. (age six):** My favorite thing about being transgender is that I'm myself now. When you're transgender, you're more yourself.

seen her waver, ever witnessed a backtracking toward boyhood, the only honest answer I can give is this: Not for a moment; not for a millisecond.

A few months ago, just shy of her thirteenth birthday, she got her blocker implant. At the time, a friend asked me if it was a tough decision, allowing my child to undergo a significant medical intervention.

"The decision was made long ago," I said. I added that it didn't really feel like a "decision," because decisions are things we make when there is more than one viable option. Thirteen-year-old girls don't *choose* to become women. They simply do, because it's who they are.

When her doctor called me with the results of her blood test ("It's time"), nearly ten years had passed since my daughter first told me that she wanted a do-over in my belly. I had been growing increasingly anxious since she started middle school, watching as she grew tall and her friends grew curvy. I didn't want to miss our moment. I didn't want to let her down, after promising for years that I would make sure she got "the medicines," after promising over and over that she would never grow a beard like her dad.

Once the tiny cylinder was inserted in her upper arm, we all breathed a big sigh of relief. And when her doctor says she's ready, she'll begin taking estrogen and will begin to look like any other teenage girl, beautiful and awkward.

Aside from the modern scientific wonder of her blocker, our own little world is, like that of my friend Lauren, notably normal.

We don't talk much about the fact that she is transgender; we're too busy just living our lives. My daughter's problems are the same ones all her teen girlfriends have: friendship drama and acne and algebra homework.

This normalcy is a rare gift. I know that she is living a life that would not be possible in the vast majority of places on this planet, where transgender people are invisible, exploited, outlawed, and too often killed or driven to take their own lives. My daughter's access to a loving, supportive community, and to legal, safe, and affordable medical care (yes, our health insurance covered her blocker) places her in a tiny and privileged category. Only the random accident of geography and timing has spared us from tragedy. This fact gives me chills and breaks my heart. And it is never far from my mind.

I am also aware of how precarious things remain. Over the past four years, I watched in horror as the trans-friendly policies put in place by the Obama administration were systematically dismantled by his successor. President Biden has begun restoring protections for people like my daughter, but I can't forget that tens of millions of Americans voted to reelect the man who rose to power on hatred and division.

While bathroom bills now, blessedly, seem to be a thing of the past, anti-trans politicians are finding new avenues to discriminate and exclude. More than one hundred anti-trans laws have been introduced so far this year, and many of them specifically target the rights of transgender youth. Thus far, nine US states have banned girls like mine from playing on girls' sports teams at school. In April, Arkansas became the first state to make it a crime for doctors to prescribe puberty blockers to trans youth. Fourteen other states have introduced similar legislation.

For now, we hang on to the good in our lives. Anna is still my daughter's beloved "big sister." She's in her early thirties and thriving in her career. M. still adores her, and recently banned me from joining their long chat on Zoom. I still rely heavily on friends from our support group, especially Alice (whose beautiful daughter Olivia just turned twenty). And I still correspond with Lauren, who is now enjoying retirement with her husband and whose emails are still filled with wholesome advice, wisdom, and hope. And although she now attends a different school, Sophie remains one of my daughter's closest friends and staunchest allies.

I still worry. About her growing up. About when she starts dating. About her traveling or moving to places where she may not be safe. About . . . everything, because I'm her mother. And when things seem too scary, I still draw strength from my daughter's fierce and bright spirit.

The morning of her scheduled procedure to insert the blocker implant, I asked her how she felt.

"Nervous and excited," she said. She explained that she was nervous because she'd be getting a shot to numb her arm. She hates needles.

"And why are you excited?" I asked.

"I'm excited to be growing up."

*JULY 2021*

# NOTES

1. Kristina Olson and Lily Durwood, "Are Parents Rushing to Turn Their Boys Into Girls?" *Slate*, January 14, 2016, slate.com/human-interest/2016/01/what-alarmist-articles-abou t-transgender-children-get-wrong.html.

2. Re: Kelvin [2017] FamCAFC 258, humanrights.gov.au/sites/default/files/Re%2BKelvin%2B30%2BNovember%2B2017.pdf.

3. Brian C. Thoma, "Suicidality Disparities Between Transgender and Cisgender Adolescents," *Pediatrics* 144, no. 5 (November 2019), pediatrics.aappublications.org/content/144/5/e20191183.

4. Colt Meier and Julie Harris, "Gender Diversity and Transgender Identity in Children," *American Psychological Association*, apadivisions.org/division-44/resources/advocacy/transgender-children.pdf.

5. Meier and Harris, "Gender Diversity and Transgender Identity in Children."

6. Jaime M. Grant, Lisa A. Mottet, and Justin Tanis, "Injustice at Every Turn: A Report of the National Transgender Discrimination Survey," *National Center for Transgender Equality*, transequality.org/sites/default/files/docs/resources/ NTDS_Exec_Summary.pdf.

7. Meier and Harris, "Gender Diversity and Transgender Identity in Children."

8. Marlo Mack, "Episode VII: THE FACTS (about transgender kids)," June 30, 2015, in *How to Be a Girl*, produced by Marlo Mack, podcast, MP3 audio, howtobeagirlpodcast.com/ episodes/episode-vii-the-facts-about-transgender-kids.

9. National Science Foundation, "Developmental psychologist receives 2018 Alan T. Waterman Award," news release no. 18-027, April 12, 2018, nsf.gov/news/news_summ. jsp?cntn_id=245107.

10. "Kristina Olson," Class of 2018, MacArthur Foundation, October 4, 2018, macfound.org/fellows/class-of-2018/ kristina-olson.

11. Alyssa Donovan, "New bill could overturn controversial transgender bathroom law," KXLY, updated May 14, 2021, kxly.com/new-bill-could-overturn-controversial-transg ender-bathroom-law.

12. Dave Philipps, "North Carolina Bans Local Anti-Discrimination Policies," *The New York Times*, March 23, 2016, nytimes.com/2016/03/24/us/north-carolina-to-limi t-bathroom-use-by-birth-gender.html.

13. Kristina R. Olson, Lily Durwood, Madeleine DeMeules, and Katie A. McLaughlin, "Mental Health of Transgender Children Who Are Supported in Their Identities," *PubMed* 137, no. 3 (March 24, 2016), pubmed.ncbi.nlm.nih. gov/26921285.

14. Initiative Measure No. 1515, I-3253.1/16 (Filed March 24, 2016), sos.wa.gov/_assets/elections/initiatives/finaltext_1083. pdf.

# RESOURCES

don't know where I'd be today without support and guidance from organizations devoted to helping families like mine. They have provided me with an ongoing source of community, information, and hope. I have leaned on others from the beginning, and I hope you will, too. When we encounter a child who breaks the gender rules as we know them, we don't have to reinvent the wheel, nor do we have to walk this path alone.

These are some of the organizations working to support children like mine and those who love them.

**TransFamilies** (transfamilies.org): Resources, support groups, workshops, and community forums for families and transgender and gender-diverse children

**Gender Spectrum** (genderspectrum.org): Resources for transgender youth and their families, including an annual family conference

**GenderCool Project** (gendercool.org): Positive stories about transgender and nonbinary youth

**Family Acceptance Project** (familyproject.sfsu.edu): Resources, research, and best practices for parents and professionals supporting trans youth

**Gender Diversity** (genderdiversity.org): Trainings for K–12 schools and other organizations serving transgender and gender-diverse children

**Welcoming Schools** (hrc.org/resources/schools): Resources for parents, classroom reading lists, best practices for schools to support LGBT youth

**GLSEN** (glsen.org): Resources and guidance for supporting LGBTQ students in K–12 education

**Campus Pride** (campuspride.org): Information, programs, and services for LGBTQ and ally students on college campuses across the United States

**The Trevor Project** (thetrevorproject.org): Crisis intervention and suicide prevention for LGBTQ young people

**TransYouth Project** (transyouthproject.org): Large-scale, national, longitudinal study of socially transitioned children

## PERMISSIONS ACKNOWLEDGMENTS

Every effort has been made to trace and contact copyright holders. If an error or omission is brought to our notice, we will be pleased to correct it in future editions of this book. For further information, please contact the publisher.

Photographs on pages 16, 83, 84: Public domain

Cartoons on pages 35, 140, 141, 143, 169, 170, 171 © Marlo Mack

Excerpt(s) from I AM JAZZ by Jessica Herthel and Jazz Jennings, text copyright © 2014 by TransKids Purple Rainbow Foundation. Used by permission of Dial Books for Young Readers, an imprint of Penguin Young Readers Group, a division of Penguin Random House LLC. All rights reserved.